# H O O P L A
# on the
# H U D S O N

## An Intimate View
## of New York's Great 1909
## Hudson-Fulton Celebration

## LINCOLN DIAMANT

### PURPLE MOUNTAIN PRESS
Fleischmanns, New York

For Rolf, and his Grandfather.
In tireless ways too numerous to list,
my wife, Joan,
made this book possible.
And for Ed and Harry, who believed.


``Special'' cannot even begin to express my appreciation to my good friends
Sandra and Peter Koppen for the translations from slightly archaic Dutch.

*Hoopla on the Hudson:*
*An Intimate View of New York's Great 1909 Hudson-Fulton Celebration*

First edition 2003

Published by
Purple Mountain Press, Ltd.
1060 Main Street, P.O. Box 309, Fleischmanns, New York 12430-0309
845-254-4062, 845-254-4476 (fax)
purple@catskill.net   http://www.catskill.net/purple

ISBN 1-930098-44-8

Library of Congress Control Number:
2003102884

Manufactured in the United States of America on acid-free paper.

5  4  3  2  1

Original negatives of most of the photographic illustrations reproduced in this book
were destroyed in the great Albany New York State Library fire on March 29, 1911.

# CONTENTS

# ILLUSTRATIONS

Frontispiece: Official Hudson-Fulton Poster.

# PROLOGUE

*John Adams found the Dutch most congenial. Here were a people who were solid and comfortable, thrifty and industrious, moral and above all learned, with more collections, exhibitions and museums than in all the rest of Europe. Their government was republican and their confederation was similar to that of the thirteen American states. "I doubt much," John wrote Abigail, "whether there is any nation of Europe more estimable than the Dutch."*

—PAGE SMITH: *John Adams* (1962)

IT WAS A TIME of relative innocence on lower Manhattan Island in the financial district. At a few minutes after noon on a blustery Thursday, September 2, 1909, a young blue-eyed securities analyst's clerk, of medium height, (his sparkling surname the same as mine) pushed his way through the crowded lobby of 33 Wall Street. Once outside the newfangled revolving door, he shook out the ribs of his conservatively oversized European umbrella and strode briskly through the rain down Broad Street towards the Commercial Cable Building. The lobby there contained the impressive offices of the Deutsch-Atlantische Telegraphen Gesellschaft—the German-Atlantic Cable Company.

At their counter, the man (it was indeed my father, Rudolph Diamant, a citizen of the Netherlands) reached into his coat pocket and, his pulse quickening a little, extracted a sheaf of forms, neatly typed in tariff-saving Dutch cable journalese. The several sheets carried a 1,200-word feature news article, addressed, press rate collect, to the Overseas Editor of the *Nieuwe Rotterdamsche Courant*, one of Europe's leading financial dailies (today, the *NRC-Handelsblad*, roughly equivalent to America's *Wall Street Journal*). Sped off to Rotterdam on the German underseas cable, Rudolph's story was only the first of his series of 16 dispatches from New York City, an honest Dutch eye reporting to Dutch readers on the civic razzmatazz surrounding the long awaited Hudson-Fulton Celebration.

"For some time now New York City has been preparing for a grand two-week long celebration on an order of magnitude not seen here before," ran the lead of Rudolph's first cabled dispatch.

7

In the weeks to come, more than 23,000 of my father's words, in 16 articles of varying lengths, would flow steadily to the *Courant* offices in Rotterdam. Translated here by Sandra and Peter Koppen, each is supplemented with pertinent extracts from the two volume 2,134-page official record of the 1909 Celebration, published in Albany a year later by the State of New York.

For more than a fortnight, Rudolph turned out Celebration coverage of which even a more seasoned newsman (or an overseas news desk back home in Holland) could be proud.

The Hudson-Fulton news reports contained in this series bore no individual's byline—such was not the newspaper's style—but all of Rudolph's articles ran on the paper's front page, and—in newsstand parlance—above the fold.[1]

Rudolph's exclusive dispatches conveyed to European readers all the enthusiastic hullabaloo in New York, both serious and lighthearted, that would accompany this extravagantly planned international event, played out against the pulsating urban tapestry of the greatest city in the world. It was clearly planned to present customarily blasé New Yorkers with a pageant the likes of which they had never seen. It also offered two friendly nations an unusual opportunity to reaffirm more than two centuries of their peaceable and highly profitable commerce.[2]

NOW, AFTER ALMOST A DECADE of joint Dutch/U.S. preparation, New York City was ready to host a massive international convocation up and down the banks of the Hudson River. Rudolph Diamant, who had already freelanced articles for the *Courant* back home, would now become its dependable "Man in New York." While still in Holland, he had secured the newspaper's commitment for 16 articles on the Celebration. It was an unusual opportunity for this energetic 23-year-old foreign correspondent manqué. And even the possibility of putting down new roots in America must have entered his mind. "This new Amsterdam," he would soon write home to his family, "is full of promise." Although the family's handed-down skill lay in diamond cutting and polishing, Rudolph had always hoped for a different career.[3]

FOR RUDOLPH DIAMANT, it had been an uneventful ten-day Atlantic crossing from Rotterdam on the pokey little 575-foot twin-screw Dutch steamer *Rijndam*.[4]

At the end of his voyage on May 26, 1909, an excited Rudolph and his jocund fellow second-class passengers, now traditionally free to roam the ship's first class areas to see whatever they may have been missing en route, gathered along the topmost starboard rail to stare in wonder at the incredible skyline, rising above the now slightly misty waters of the upper bay like a 1909 Camelot-on-the-Hudson. The New York harbor pilot rang for "AHEAD SLOW" as he guided the *Rijndam* through a skein of smaller vessels in what was undoubtedly the finest port city in the world. The ship steamed smoothly across New York's Upper Bay, past that incredible icon, the 500-foot-high statue of "Liberty Enlightening the World, steering towards the Holland-America Line's (Nederlandsche-Ameri-kaansche Stoomvaart-Maatschappij) Hoboken piers. Many *Rijndam* passengers may have read Emma Lazarus's classic poem, dedicated to "Lady Liberty," and sounding America's traditional welcome, "I lift my lamp beside the golden door." (In the *Rijndam* engine room, the ship's telegraph finally rang, "FINISHED WITH ENGINES." The sea trip was over, and Rudolph was in Hoboken, New Jersey, across the Hudson River from New York City. He would soon be required to profess to the satisfaction of an immigration inspector a formal abjuration of the twin turn-of-the-century evils of anarchy and polygamy, and attest that he had at least $50 in his pocket. Everything else was just beginning.

RUDOLPH soon found himself swallowed up by the "great melting pot."[5]

Romantic schoolboy visions of one day becoming a famous globe-trotting reporter, accomplishing feats of journalistic daring-do, must surely have danced in Rudolph's mind. There can be little doubt that the "Courant" editorial board ran some risk in assigning this international reportage to a newswriter with Rudolph's lack of real experience. But the *Courant* was not being charitable. As Benjamin Franklin once remarked, "Of what use is a baby?" The editors saw promise in the young man's intelligence and self-possession. Rudolph, too, never doubted that he would be able to cover the entire fortnight's assignment.

However, when it came to earning a living, he was a realist. Immediately awaiting him ashore was a completely different, and comparatively unexciting, dollars-and-cents job, negotiated weeks earlier through the London branch of H. W. Poor and Company, an important Wall Street securities firm. It was only an entry level position as a bilingual statistical clerk.[6]

Poor's business was based on their publication of a number of important investment "Manuals" filled with statistical data, supplying materials for abstracts covering major areas of commercial and industrial investment. As the U.S. economy boomed after that "splendid little [Spanish-American] war," as John Hay[7] described the successful 88-day conflict, Poor's essential investment guides pointed the way to a rational appraisal of world markets. Long before the age of computers, from almost every page of these manuals, investment opportunities beckoned. The accepted international epicenter for all this financial and mercantile activity was the incredibly magnetic city of New York, now preparing to strut its stuff with a historic world-class exposition. In so many ways, New York was an extraordinary metropolis, ready for expositions and exhibitions, come what may, 365 days a year. As an article of faith for most New Yorkers, the Greek *omphalus*, the Delphic "navel of the world", had now been transferred to the intersection of Fifth Avenue and 42nd Street. There, motor vehicles, limited to a speed of 20 miles an hour, had their movements completely choreographed by a traffic policeman in a glass booth 25 feet above the pavement. In his transparent coop, he waved a set of green and red paddles to control the unending flow of automobiles, taxicabs, crosstown trolley cars, horses, wagons, and pedestrians. There was nothing like it anywhere in Holland or in Europe. New York City was clearly on the move!

IN THE POOR'S OFFICE, Rudolph was assigned a bottom place on the employment totem pole. His five-and-a-half-day work week was jammed with humdrum low-level statistical computations and compilations using a trusty hand-driven Monroe calculator. In his uncomfortably hot little Wall Street cubicle, tiny but uncluttered, he worked in shirt-sleeves, patiently crunching a universe of numbers on his Monroe machine while awaiting every day's hour of deliverance. Then, like Superman in reverse, he would whip into the proper Clark Kent guise of a brash young Dutch reporter, dispatched to these shores to chronicle the mammoth Hudson-Fulton Celebration, as the spectacle unfolded in and around the city and far up the Hudson Valley.

FORTUNATELY FOR RUDOLPH, most of the major events of the Celebration were held either at night or during the weekends, which fit neatly into his Poor's working schedule, although some hooky-playing was probably necessary. Despite his apparent ability to be in two places at once, he did miss Wilbur Wright's exciting demonstrations in his new *Flyer*.

WITH TOTAL COOPERATION from the Dutch government, who were probably more bemused than surprised, the Hudson-Fulton Celebration turned out to be a massive glowing fete that every citizen of New York enthusiastically enjoyed. All the exciting days and sparkling nights that lay ahead would be filled with colorful orations (some pontifical), clever costumed and singing marches, a great number of decorative floats with historic and literary tableaux, ceremonial banquets, dazzling illuminations, blockbuster parades, a fleet of foreign and U.S. warships, replicas of historic vessels, and even the promise of newfangled "air races" between the Wright brothers' *Flyer*, and their arch rival, former motorcycle racer Glenn Curtiss's 1908 *June Bug*—all in the span of only 16 days! New York City had never seen, or imagined, anything like it. What a show! The citizens of New York were almost as agog as the young Dutch reporter.

The event, christened by its civic organizers as "The Hudson-Fulton Celebration," actually conflated two major anniversaries from America's historic past. One was the 1609 voyage up and down the Hudson River by the English explorer and his doughty (some would say, murderous) crew aboard the tiny *Halve-*

*Maen* ("Half-Moon") on their epochal voyage of North American discovery. The "other half" of the Celebration, which received an obviously shorter shrift from the Dutch participants, commemorated Robert Fulton's 1807 introduction of passenger and freight steamboat service on the Hudson River. Fulton's route covered 150 miles between New York City and the state capital at Albany. The correct historical dates were known to all; their eventual combination, although it ruffled a few feathers, was merely a realistic way to help keep the Celebration solvent.[8]

THE 1909 HUDSON-FULTON FESTIVITIES followed in grand style the tradition of jubilant international fairs and exhibitions that had begun a half century earlier with London's 1851 cast-iron-and-glass Crystal Palace Exposition. The varied presentations were mainly served "under glass," so to speak. They included displays of industrial and cultural achievements, exhibits of the arts and handicrafts, food and entertainment. It became a typical mix for all international fairs to copy. The United States followed in 1876 with the Philadelphia Centennial Exhibition, honoring the American Revolution and the century of social, industrial, and economic expansion that came after. Thirteen years later, the great Paris Exhibition (with A. G. Eiffel's remarkable 984-foot tower) won worldwide notice and acclaim, and donated an enduring symbol to Parisian life. In 1893, a year late for the 400th anniversary of Columbus's landing, Chicago was literally electrified by the Columbian Exposition's incandescent "Great White City."[9] Hard on the heels of the Chicago event came the St. Louis Exposition of 1904.

THE NEW YORK HUDSON-FULTON CELEBRATION was planned to be different from all of them. Instead of enclosing the exhibition in a series of great weatherproof glass-roofed halls, it would use the entire city and its picturesque Hudson River as a stage, subject, of course, to the vagaries of fall winds and rain. It would also be concentrated in time, from Saturday, September 25, to Monday, October 4, plus some additional days, north of the city, for restaged events.

The American and Dutch Celebration commissioners arranged their plans with definite ends in view. Most important of these was their final decision that all events and presentations would be "educational," with care taken to avoid anything of too obvious a commercial nature. Sobeit.

How well this policy trickled down can be best judged by some of Rudolph's earliest reactions. He noted that no advertising was permitted in the great parades; no advertisements appeared in the official literature; no admission fee was charged for any function upon which city or state public monies had been expended; and no public monies were expended on any personal decorations or souvenirs for the members of the Commission or others, excepting keepsake bronze medallions. This great free celebration was purposely designed to be as educational as possible with assurance that the largest number of spectators, old and young, could view and enjoy the different events.

**Plate 1: Official Hudson-Fulton Celebration seal.**

In addition, the Hudson-Fulton Celebration would present a shining spectacle to other nations, offering a full fortnight of grandiose New World pageantry while the rest of the world was busily entangling itself in two great political and military alliances.

The unprecedented civic illuminations called for stringing New York's nighttime streets and avenues (and even the sides of its skyscrapers) with festoons and clusters of glowing incandescent bulbs like cranberry chains on a Christmas tree.

WHERE DID IT ALL START? The concept of holding a citywide Henry Hudson tricentennial celebration was contained in a July 31, 1893, letter to the editor of the *New-York Tribune* from Reverend J. H. Suydam, a clergyman of solid Dutch extraction living in Rhinecliff, N.Y.[10]

In it the clergyman proposed a belated fin de siècle commemoration paying special honor to the 55-year long Dutch chapter of North America's early history. Following Reverend Suydam's suggestion, the New York's St. Nicholas and Holland Societies soon found themselves jointly undertaking initial responsibility for staffing such a festivity.

From the start, planning called for the participation of almost every major organization and society in the five boroughs of the 301-square-mile metropolis. A problem lay in the difficulty of orchestrating all those strident tribal chants into a single marvelous "Manificat."

Progress at first was agonizingly slow. After eight years of procrastination, the Holland Society finally moved off the dime, appointing chairmen for all the key Celebration committees. They were drawn from the membership of eight important civic groups, with the Metropolitan Museum of Art's president J. Piermont Morgan, as chairman of the Celebration's Art and Historical Exhibits Committee. By June 1902, a small band of hardy members of the Holland Society reorganized under a new title: The Hudson Tricentennial Association, with offices in the *Tribune* building on Park Row, across from City Hall. The Association welcomed under its single roof groups as diverse as the American Scenic Preservation Society, the Sons of the American Revolution, the Municipal Arts Society, the National Arts Club, the New York Society of the Order of the Founders and Patriots of America, and the Saint Nicholas Society. Everyone realized that New York was on the edge of something very big. And amity prevailed.

To the American committee's ranks were eventually added the impressive family names of Roosevelt, Stillman, Carnegie, Vanderbilt, Rockefeller,[11] and—in the fullness of time—Mark Twain. With the influx of 150 new American committee members that were appointed by the Commission's chairman—a strong organizer, General Stewart L. Woodford (USA Ret.),[12] the Celebration got underway.

The first order of business on the seven-year construction schedule was a memorial parkway bridge spanning Spuyten Duyvil Creek and connecting the City's Manhattan and Bronx Counties, and opening up the highroad to Yonkers.[13]

A floodlit 106-foot-high fluted granite column was planned for the center of the bridge's north plaza. It was to be surmounted by a 16-foot-high bronze statue of Henry Hudson, peering anxiously down the river (perhaps in search of some future bellicose parks commissioner?). Inside, the column was hollow, with a set of iron rungs affording emergency access to the top. The planning went forward with a generous contribution from William C. Muschenheim.[14]

The Hudson statue was commissioned to the noted sculptor Karl Bitter, who died in an automobile accident six years later, with the column complete but the statue still in work. After Bitter's death, his student Karl H. Gruppe was awarded responsibility for completing the sculpture and executing two new bas-reliefs at the base of the column. But still missing were Bitter's original sketches and a three-foot-high plaster model of the statue. Gruppe finally unearthed a photo-

graph of the plaster maquette, on
which all his remaining efforts
would be based. By then, the
funds originally allocated to the
bridge and plaza project had been
distributed under various other
headings.

A quarter of a century later, in
1936, with the completion of the
Henry Hudson Bridge and
Parkway, Parks Commissioner
Moses decided to have the memorial statue finished and placed
atop the existing column, as originally planned. But it was not until
January 6, 1938, that the 4-ton statue of Hudson was finally hoisted
to its lofty perch.

Today, the Henry Hudson
Memorial Column, surrounded by
dozens of condominiums, stands
in   magnificent   isolation   in
Riverdale's tiny Henry Hudson
pocket park on Independence
Avenue. Parkway motorists can
still catch a fleeting glimpse of
Hudson on his aerie as their automobiles hurtle by.

AS TO THE FULTON SIDE of the 1909
Celebration, the suggestion was
made in 1902 to have the city mark
the centenary of Robert Fulton's
first steamboat trip up the Hudson
in 1807. The concept slowly surfaced like one of Fulton's early
submarines, once offered to, and
rejected by, the French Admiralty.
The result was the spectacle of two

**Plate 2: Henry Hudson monument
(unfinished).**

competing organizations memorializing two heroes in two different and expensive venues. The nifty idea of combining the two still took considerable jockeying and discussion before it was agreed that the name and activities of the Fulton group would be subsumed under the new name of the "Hudson-Fulton Celebration."

AS FOR RUDOLPH, he found himself in New York with only three and a half months to thoroughly familiarize himself with the city and prepare for his dual role as journalist and low level statistical clerk. Attempting to master all the nuances of a language that was not his own, he did well. Each day he set forth from his 30 Elm Avenue boarding house in the Flatbush section of Brooklyn, or his Manhattan office building, and became a dedicated and footloose walker in the city, as well as a fearless explorer of New York's intricate BMT or IRT subway system, and the older but still pleasant elevated—"El"—trains. Wandering through bustling neighborhoods, savoring ethnic variety, he recorded his impressions. All of the metropolis's gaudy preparations for the big Hudson-Fulton show, some artistic, some tasteless and tawdry, were carefully noted. Despite Rudolph's occasional chiding of the host city's sense of history, he was always gentle, never argumentative. According to later friends and colleagues, he was able to see American life, with all its imperfections, pretty much as it was, displaying no rancor or incivility. Ignoring many of his own deeply held social beliefs, he saw himself as a qualified interpreter of this complicated celebration. For him, the lodestone of the "sweet Land of Liberty" remained the City of New York. Perhaps it was inevitable that he would stay on in the United States, working at Poor's, long after all the hoopla on the Hudson had become memory.

With some misgivings, he decided to forsake the quiet of Amsterdam's tree-lined canals for the hurly-burly existence of a New Yorker. He applied for citizenship, and found himself a 23-year-old winsome, dark-eyed, year-younger American bride who worked as a sculptor in the studio of Gutzon Borglum.[15] After several years of marriage, they suffered the grievous loss of the firstborn of their three sons. I was the youngest.

AS A WALL STREET PROFESSIONAL, Rudolph's progress up the traditional American economic ladder was slow but steady. Before long—at a time when Congress was actively flirting with nationalizing America's railroads—Rudolph was working as a railroad bond analyst for the Prudential, one of America's largest insurance companies. It was a worthy challenge, bringing him into daily contact with the United States' railroad industry. From time to time, gathering extra material for Poor's Railroad Manual, he would travel in wide swings across his adopted country, flashing his coveted golden pass issued by the Association of American Railroads, and rating for investment purposes, the quality of a line's rolling stock, rights-of-way values, including maintenance of comfortable passenger cars, loco-motives, fueling costs, real estate holdings, and local competition. On occasion, from his Pullman window, he became an unexpected witness to rough-and-tum-ble encounters between railroad security personnel and a horde of ragged, home-less and footloose hoboes and drifters, mainly veterans of World War I, criss-crossing the United States in empty boxcars in search of any kind of employment. Following the bitter railroad strikes that almost brought the United States to its knees at the turn of the century, it was now a boom time and Rudolph's reports were generally positive. People began to notice.

# IN THE YEAR: 1909

*O wonder! How many goodly creatures are there here! How beau-teous is mankind! O brave new world that has such people in't!*
—Act V, THE TEMPEST

BESIDES THE HUDSON-FULTON CELEBRATION, what were American newsmen reporting on in New York City and elsewhere in 1909, almost a decade into the new century?

Severe financial panics had followed the Civil War, and the nation had not yet fully extricated itself from the sink and stink of social and economic corruption that characterized what Mark Twain dubbed "the Gilded Age."

After shameful international delays, the late 19th century foresaw the final extirpation of the infamous international African slave trade. It had been an abomination of abominations. In the world's affected areas, the slaves' muscle power was slowly being replaced by local canals, steamboats, railways, and inter-nal combustion engines, all tied together by almost miraculous advances in com-munications.

People were living in a whirlwind of change.

FOR ALMOST A QUARTER CENTURY, from her granite perch in New York's Upper Bay, Bartholdi's colossal copper-clad statue of "Liberty Enlightening the World" had been beckoning millions of immigrants and visitors to these shores and a bet-ter life. Among them were more than a few poor Dutch farming families, seeking new agricultural opportunities in the American Midwest, with thousands taking up land in what was to become Holland, Michigan.

The United States was now a country with 90 million people (in my own life-time, that figure has more than doubled), 16 million had swarmed from abroad during the past ten years. By 1898, New York had overtaken Greater London as the most populous city in the world. Nothing but glory days shone ahead.

In the spring of 1909, the U.S. Navy's "Great White Fleet" triumphantly returned from showing the flag to nations around the world. The last U.S. soldiers were wrapping up their long military occupation of Cuba; later in the year they would be transported to Nicaragua. For five years, the Americans had been steam-shov-eling away at their own new and improved version of the (originally French) design for the Panama Canal—"A man, a plan, a canal: Panama"! Five more years of difficult construction on this icon of early 20th century civil engineering lay ahead. Admiral Robert Peary and Dr. Frederick Cook and their vociferously deri-sive supporters were stepping up a bitter war of accusations as to which man had been the first to set foot on latitude 90º north—the North Pole. At the same time in Antarctica, Ernest Shackleton and his expedition reached a point within 88º south latitude (97 miles) of the South Pole, before turning back. Conservative Republican William Howard Taft of Ohio was in his first year in the White House. Somewhere between a joke and a symbol, the new president's unusual obesity forced the White House plumbers of an earlier day to fabricate (and pose in) a special oversize bathtub. Taft had replaced Theodore Roosevelt, who was now leading a Smithsonian charge killing elephants in Kenya. E. V. Debs, the U.S. Socialist Party's perennial presidential candidate, polled almost half a million votes, compared to Taft's seven and a half million and William Jennings Bryan's six and a half million. In this single kaleidoscopic year, small-town America was enjoying a period of relative prosperity. The Dow-Jones stock index rewarded 1909 investors with an overall gain for the entire year of 12.9 points! The Senate submitted the 16th Constitutional Amendment to the 46 states to institute an annual tax on American personal income. Less than half the nation possessed even a grade school education; child labor was ubiquitous—not only in the south-ern states. Near Cherry in downstate Illinois, 259 miners were asphyxiated in a coal mine explosion. Almost anticipating Prohibition, east coast hop growing was nearly wiped out by a devastating "blue mold" epidemic. Orville Wright posted a one-hour endurance record; back on the ground, he and brother Wilbur launched an eight-year patent infringement lawsuit against Glenn Curtiss, their *ab ovo* rival. Another Wright, Frank Lloyd the architect, designed and built Chicago's landmark Robie House. An electronic message was flashed from New York to Chicago without wires.

Henry Ford's Detroit assembly line produced more than 19,000 Model Ts at $825 each; none had a self-starter. You cranked and occasionally broke your arm. All Fords were painted black. The first plastic, named "Bakelite" by its inventor Leo Baekeland, popped out of its thermosetting mold. The underground (and underwater) New York subway system, already the largest in the world, now linked three of "Greater New York's" five consolidated (1898) boroughs. The city was close to completing a major addition to its fabulous Croton water supply: a huge new reservoir in the Catskill Mountains, with its 130-mile-long Ashokan aqueduct delivering more than one billion gallons of drinking water to New York City every day. Two grand new bridges, the Williamsburg and the Queensboro, were opened to span New York's East River (the Roeblings' earlier engineering triumph had been carrying pedestrian and vehicular traffic across the river from Brooklyn to Manhattan for more than 25 years).

The less than a dozen artists in the so-called "Ashcan" school of contemporary American painting continued to increase their public recognition and acceptance through small group exhibitions. Ezra Pound published his first book of literary criticism. Hearst newspaper cartoonist Richard *"Yellow Kid"* Outcault, "father of the comic strip," widened his *"Buster Brown"* image franchising across the country. GE launched the electric toaster. Sigmund Freud lectured at Worcester, Massachusetts. "Wintergreen," with J. Powers aboard, won the Kentucky Derby, going away. W. C. Handy composed the "Memphis Blues," originally as a political campaign song for "Boss" Crump of that Tennessee city. Buddy Bolden, an esteemed New Orleans jazzman, was permanently committed to a mental institution. Winsor McCay inked the first American black-and-white animated film, the 10-minute cartoon "Gertie the Dinosaur." Harvard-educated W. E. B. Du Bois founded the NAACP to spearhead the struggle for African-American civil rights. Jack London dashed off his autobiographical "Martin Eden." The American Red Cross sold its first sheet of "Christmas Seals" to help combat tuberculosis. And as the Hudson-Fulton Celebration came to an end, Pittsburgh beat Detroit in the sixth annual World Series.

TO THE REST OF THE GLOBE, Americans in this magnetic city appeared to be living the good life, with labor's contributions writ small and the achievements of finance capital writ large. For such a wonderful country, not every one of its systems during the period 1865 to 1908 was functioning ideally. Rudolph's objective eye reflected many of these contradictions, with occasional flashes of nationalist—and even self-deprecating—wit.

Only the bitterest soothsayer could have suggested that the Hudson-Fulton Celebration would be the last of such international events until Chicago's 1933 World's Fair. In less than five years, the so-called "civilized" nations of the world, urged on by blatherskite generals and admirals from both sides, would plunge much of the globe into a brutal war that premiered the use of Maxim machine guns and poison gas. The war quickly became a conflict of unprecedented, almost indescribable savagery, interrupted near its end by rare moments of front line fraternization and mutiny (the French general staff, true to form, reacted by executing its own rebellious *poilus*). One result of this "Great" war: 14,000,000 deaths.

THIS IS A STORY whose chronological timeline reaches back through the centuries. It is now almost 100 years since my father, reflecting emotions running from enthusiasm to apprehension, came striding down the *Rijndam* gangplank. As I began to put this story together, sifting through half-forgotten news clippings, journals, notes, and translations, I found myself weighing all the thoughts that must have gone racing through Rudolph's mind when he was forced to choose between a financial or journalistic career. Was it simply a "bird in the hand," or a fork in the road? Whatever it was, it made all the difference.

As I learned about Rudolph's earliest jobs on Wall Street, I remembered the occasional agonies and triumphs of my own whippersnapper career in the advertising business, at McCann-Erickson, Grey Advertising, and Ogilvy & Mather. The employment path I so doggedly pursued might have amused, or dismayed, my father.

In the rightness of everything (or nothing), it was perhaps inevitable that I be assigned to shepherd the television commercial advertising fortunes of Shell gasoline. Royal Dutch Shell, that is. To each his own.[16]

NOW RETIRED, with sorely diminished eyesight, but with the assistance of some remarkable 21st-century electronic gadgets, I find enormous satisfaction studying and writing about American history and the American Revolution in particular. Like my father before me, I have marveled at the Hudson and its magnificent river valley.

All my life I have made my home within two miles of this great, beautiful and historic river. I have plied my way through its waters in every type of craft from a folding kayak to the magnificent floating palaces of the old Day Line. Discovering that my father, too, had admired the same water and terrain creates new connections with a man I barely knew. I interweave his articles, translated from a now somewhat archaic Dutch, with my own explanatory footnotes and comments, augmented where possible or necessary with citations from the official record, and by my own biographical sketches of the two men whose curiosity and persistence led the way to the 1909 celebration—Captain Henry Hudson and Captain Robert Fulton.

*Pondside*
*Ossining, New York*

# NOTES

[1]Sole exception, to fill out the big Celebration picture, was Reuters' coverage, which told the local story from Wilmington/Lewes, Delaware.

[2] In 1776, the Netherlands, only recently emerged from their own long struggle for independence from Spain, was the first country to recognize the new government of the United States of America and salute its warships. On November 16, 1776, Fort Orange on the Dutch West Indies island of St. Eustatius exchanged cannon salutes with the American warship *Andrew Doria*.

[3]A brief genealogical digression: Rudolph Diamant was born in Amsterdam on April 16, 1887, to assimilated but unconverted lower middle class Sephardic parents whose emigrant ancestry could be traced back to the Spanish Diaspora at the end of the 15th century. His father was Nathan Diamant (born September 4, 1854); his mother was Maria Vliekruijer (born December 10, 1853). Rudolph's siblings included a younger sister and six brothers—Mark, Philip, Adolph, Joop, Bernard, and Solomon.

[4]Built for the Holland-America Line by a Belfast shipyard in 1901, the Rijndam carried 2,282 passengers; 196 first class, 286 second class, 1,800 third class. It was converted to a World War I American troopship in 1918, and scrapped in 1929.

In 1909 the era of swift and luxurious passenger service across the Atlantic had not yet arrived (although the indestructible keel plates for a behemoth of a steamship named *Titanic* were already resting on a Belfast slipway. (It would soon become the largest moveable man-made object on earth.)

[5]The famous image created a few years earlier by the noted Zionist playwright Israel Zangwil.

[6]In the 1940s, Poor's merged with the Standard Statistics Company to create Standard & Poor's Corporation, the research and rating service, now owned by McGraw-Hill, that developed the  bellwether "S&P 500" securities index.

[7]United States Secretary of State under Presidents William McKinley and Theodore Roosevelt.

[8]The only significant event in the Fulton chronology for the year 1809 was a historic legal action that eventually led to the dissolution—by John Marshall and the United States Supreme Court—of Fulton's asserted steamboat monopoly over every navigable waterway in the United States.

[9]The electric light bulb had been invented 16 years earlier in Thomas A. Edison's New Jersey laboratory.

[10]A riverside village in the upper Hudson Valley.

[11]Across the Hudson, within eyesore view of *Kykuit*, (the Rockefeller Family compound at Pocantico Hills), a dozen large and small traprock quarries relentlessly gnawed away at one of the great geologic landmarks of the world, the Hudson River Palisades. Before long, plans to preserve these ancient cliffs were running hand in hand with those for the Hudson-Fulton festivities. The official dedication ceremony at Alpine New Jersey for the 37-mile-long linear park stretching from Fort Lee to Fort Montgomery, with a vertiginous path along the ridgelines, was timed to coincide with the opening of the Celebration. It

was named the Palisades Interstate [New York and New Jersey] Park.

[12]General Woodford served under William Tecumseh Sherman, and commanded several thousand African-American U.S. Army troops occupying Charleston, South Carolina at the end of the Civil War in 1865.

[13]Construction of the Henry Hudson Bridge (as part of the West Side/Henry Hudson Parkway) was delayed until the 1930s and the era of the memorable New York City Parks Commissioner Robert Moses. When finally completed, the bridge used a revised alignment.

[14]Owner/manager of the five-star Hotel Astor in Manhattan, Muschenheim was also the owner of the Riverdale estate through which the projected parkway was to pass and on which the proposed memorial column would be erected.

[15]Creator of the four huge presidential heads carved into Mount Rushmore in South Dakota.

[16]A 1986 memoir, "Playing the Shell Game" in Chicago's *Advertising Age* so enraged the Windy City's O&M staffers that they threatened to roast me at the stake.

# CHAPTER I

# 400 Years Ago: HENRY HUDSON

*If you see a stranger come by the side of your fireplace, you must be friendly to him—for you, too, will be a stranger one day.*
—PRECEPT OF THE (Hudson River)
MUHHEAKUNNUK NATION

LET US BEGIN this saga with Captain Hudson and his long 1609 voyage of exploration aboard the *Halve-Maen*, named for the arc-shaped canals of its home port, the Dutch city of Amsterdam.

By the middle of the 16th century, huge and clumsy white-winged European vessels were not unknown to the Muhheakunnuk natives living near the Atlantic coast. Carracks and caravels, pinnaces and grand galleons, homeward bound from looting the Indies, Mexico, and Central America, would occasionally sail by the offshore sandbars, blown northward from their trade wind course.

But the mouth of the great Mahicanituck river seemed to hold little interest for any of these strange ships. Only once, in the early 1500s, an Italian sailing for a French king briefly threaded the Sandy Hook shoals that guarded its half-hidden yet spacious harbor.

Entering the River of the Steep Hills, we found the countrymen on its banks had covered themselves with the feathers of birds of various colors. They came towards us with evident delight, raising loud shouts of admiration, rowing 30 or more of their small boats from one shore to another, filled with multitudes who came to see us. But all of a sudden, a violent contrary wind blew in, and forced us to leave this region which seemed so commodious and delightful.

Giovanni da Verrazano never returned to the great harbor he discovered, but the legend of his peaceful visit was mingled with ten centuries of tribal lore of the Muhheakunnuk people.

Eighty-five years later, another vessel tacked north against a contrary breeze into the broad estuary. It was the tiny *Halve-Maen*, captained by English Henry Hudson on a disorderly voyage of exploration with shoestring underwriting from a huge Dutch trading company.

THE STORY of those crucial first encounters between the *Halve-Maen*'s crew and the Muhheakunnuk "River Indians" must rely on only two eye-witness accounts, both published independently—in England and Holland—16 years after Hudson's voyage. Any other record that existed has disappeared forever into the dustbin of history.

By 1841, when New York State officially sought to recover from Holland additional Dutch East and West Indies Companies' documents dealing with the discovery and settlement of New Netherland, the Dutch government had just auctioned them off, scattering the pertinent papers. Nothing new on Hudson's explorations, or on Hudson himself, has ever surfaced. One may assume that the priceless relics were used either to wrap herring or to light fires.

But in 1625, Hudson's own now-lost journal lay open in Leyden, in front of Johannes de Laet, an eminent geographer and director of the newly formed Nederlandsche West-Indische Compagnie—the Dutch West India Company.[1]

He was laboring over Nieuwee Wereld, his monumental real estate promotion of all the knowledge of North America brought back by early explorers. Part of de Laet's tenth chapter actually quoted Henry Hudson. They are the only direct words we can ever expect from this irresolute visionary, the superb navigator who captained tiny, scummy, pocky crews to the farthest reaches of the North Atlantic, accommodating mutiny after mutiny until the final uprising that put a theatrically frozen end to his life.

WE HAVE a second, lengthier account of the voyage of 1609 from Robert Juet, "an olderman," perhaps an officer on the *Halve-Maen*, perhaps even Hudson's first mate, although he never tells us his rank or role on the fateful trip. It was this same Juet who two years later (June 22, 1611) put Hudson and his son overboard in the icy waters now known as Hudson's Bay. Yet there is no whisper of mutiny on any page of Juet's slim, straightforward journal of the *Halve-Maen*'s erratic, querulous search on behalf of the new and already fabulously wealthy Dutch East India Company for some shortened route to the cloves and spices of the Molucca Islands.

Their zigzag path went north to the Arctic, then southwest to the present coast of Maine, south again (out of sight of land) to Virginia, then north along the Atlantic seacoast, and into and up the great river of Hudson's discovery.

ESCAPING THE CRIMPS and whores who patrolled the quays and wharves of Amsterdam, and flying the old orange, white, and blue flag of the United Provinces, the *Halve-Maen* set sail on 4 April 1609 ("novo stile," Juet carefully tells us, for the radical Gregorian calendar had now come into use). The small craft passed swiftly through the North Sea and up the Norwegian coast towards Novaya Zemlya and the chimerical "northeast passage." Hudson had proclaimed to his Dutch sponsors that this shortcut could trim three to six thousand miles off the long and vulnerable spice route around the Cape of Good Hope or through the Straits of Magellan.

But week after week of fruitless tacking through foggy, ice-choked Arctic waters whipped Hudson's tiny unmanageable crew—20 polyglot castoffs crimped from the wharves of one of the world's largest port cities—to a frenzied, mutinous halt. There was "much lack of goodwill among the crew," Emmanuel van Meeteren, Dutch Consul in London, would report five months later. They forced their Master to turn the *Halve-Maen* southwest towards warmer seas, presumably to seek an alternate "northwest passage" in a different hemisphere.

Three months after leaving home, they all sailed silently (and perhaps nervously) through a great French fishing fleet on the Grand Banks off Nova Scotia. "We spake with none of them," reports Juet. Thirteen days later, on 16 July, the adventurers made their American landfall in the bay of the Penobscot, the native name for "the river that falls from a height." The following day, "savages of the country" came out in the fog in two canoes to visit the Dutch ship. One of the native visitors even spoke French.


ALTHOUGH EUROPEANS had been in close contact with Native Americans for more than half a century, few exploring parties ever demonstrated a more momentous paranoia than that possessing the *Halve-Maen*'s rebellious, easily outnumbered crew. Their fear and contempt would afflict relations with the native peoples they encountered for more than half a century. "The people coming alongside showed us great friendship but we could not trust them."

Again and again Robert Juet voices this fright. Although events would shortly suggest who could trust whom, at the moment all seemed friendly: "Two boats full of country people came into the harbor, bringing many beaver skins and other fine furs, which they would have changed for red gowns; the French trade with them for red cassocks."

The *Halve-Maen*'s trading goods included no cassocks; the disappointed natives paddled away. But the avaricious crew could not relax. "We kept good watch, for fear of being betrayed by the country people."

The following day the crew took one of the rowboats and spent the morning in a desultory attempt to trade with the natives, who now refused to meet them face to face. They insisted on exchanging goods by use of a long rope from the top of a nearby cliff. When this unsatisfactory exchange was concluded, the natives mooned the crew as the latter rowed away.

And on 5 July Juet adds this disquieting report: "With twelve men and muskets, we drove the savages from their houses and took the spoil of them, as they would have done of us."

FROM THE COLD waters of the Maine coast, Hudson and his freebooters turned southward, skirting Cape Cod and heading directly toward the Virginia Capes, newly settled by Hudson's old friend and fellow explorer, John Smith. Here Hudson came about without any onshore visit and made their way northward, eschewing any possibility of a "northwest passage" in broad Delaware Bay. They avoided further intercourse with native inhabitants along the coast until they finally arrived inside Sandy Hook on September 4, apparently only the second group of European explorers to enter New York Harbor after almost one hundred years.

During 20 of the next 28 days, Hudson and his crew were in contact with the Muhheakunnuk people along the river, days marked by fear, kidnapping, and bloodshed, only occasionally interspersed with the vision of peaceful coexistence. The geographer Johannes de Laet was later able to extract from Hudson's journal: "sufficient reason for us to conclude from the explorer's mixed accounts that. . .with mild and proper treatment, and especially by intercourse with Christians, this people might be civilized and brought under better regulation."

For his part, mate Juet described the initial Muhheakunnuk welcome: "The people of the country came alongside, seeming very glad of our coming, and brought green tobacco and gave it to us for knives and beads. They go in deerskins, loose, well-dressed. They have yellow copper. They desire clothes, and are very civil. They have a great store of maize or Indian wheat, whereof they make good bread . . ." It must have seemed like the new Jerusalem. "At night they went on land again, so we rode very quiet. But we durst not trust them."

Two days later, Hudson sent his shallop[2] with five men to explore Newark Bay. There they encountered the long-feared violence. Juet is closemouthed; the sailors had been at sea six months (not counting the Penobscot foray) and one can only speculate on the possibility of sexual misadventure ashore, away from the sober Master's eye. Unlike some aborigines in other parts of the New World, the Muhheakunnuk did not proffer their women to exploring strangers, but did all possible to maintain their chastity.

The *Halve-Maen*'s shallop was hotly pursued by 26 natives in two long canoes, digging deeply with their paddles. John Colman, an English sailor commanding the scouting party, received an arrow in his throat. Two other sailors were wounded, after the firing match for their muskets, a smoldering wick, was extinguished by a sudden squall. In the rain, the party made good their escape and spent the night drifting with the tides around Staten Island, watching Colman die.

They rejoined their ship at sunrise; Colman was buried on the beach at Sandy Hook. The *Halve-Maen*'s shallop was quickly converted into a miniature warship, its sides built up with spare planks to protect against further arrows. The next day, when the natives returned to trade, bringing "tobacco and Indian wheat to exchange for knives and beads, and offering us no violence, they were purposely shown the fortified shallop to see if they would make any show of the death of our man, which they did not."

The following day, more traditional European social interchange began in earnest. "Two great canoes came alongside, full of men to betray us, but we perceived their intent. We took two of them, to have kept them, and put red coats on them, and would not suffer the others to come near us. We kept the one and let the second go, but he which we had taken, got up and leapt overboard."

The saltwater "northwest passage" still beckoned; the *Halve-Maen*'s crew sailed north into Upper Bay on 11 September. "The people of the country came alongside, and gave us tobacco and Indian wheat, making show of love. But we durst not trust them."

The following day, off the northern end of Manhattan Island "there came eight and twenty canoes full of men, women and children to betray us. But we saw their intent, and suffered none of them to come aboard." The "betrayal" party, Juet adds "brought with them oysters and beans, whereof we bought some." And four miles north on the spacious river "there came four canoes alongside, but we suffered none of them to come into our ship. They brought a great store of very good oysters, which we bought for trifles."

Sometime between 9-14 September, two other natives were kidnapped by the explorers. Whether it was for slavery, trophy, or amusement, one cannot say. But any possible native reaction to the abduction may have seemed unimportant to Hudson; after all, every sounding he made in the shallow but still reassuringly wide salt waters of the great river, nourished the conviction that he was now indeed sailing on his way to the Spice Islands, with nary a step to retrace. Off Croton Point on the 15th, the kidnapped natives managed to escape through a porthole, Juet complains "and swam away. And after we were under sail, they called to us in scorn."

THE *HALVE-MAEN* was blown—or laboriously tacked—up a crooked stretch of what would shortly prove (with a jolt) to be no passage at all, but a unique and deceptive 150-mile long fjord of the northeast coastline. But when Hudson discovered the bottom dropping off slightly over glacial debris that choked its 175-foot-deep course through the Highlands, he felt certain that he had finally located the legendary ice-free intercontinental strait.

It was a resplendent time of year on Hudson's river, with hints of strange and glorious colors still to come to the huge hardwood trees that lined its banks. The *Halve-Maen* was now well upstream under crisp and clear autumn skies, in the land of the Muhheakunnuk Wappinger Nation: "The people came alongside and brought us ears of Indian corn, pumpkins and tobacco, which we bought for trifles."

Two days later, Hudson, trading on their ignorance of his tense downriver encounters "went on land with an old savage, a governor of the country, who carried him to his house and made him good cheer."

From Johannes de Laet's transcription from Hudson's log, the Master himself picks up his lost narrative of the visit with the Wappinger sachem:

> I sailed to the shore in one of their canoes, with an old man, who was chief of a tribe consisting of 40 men and 17 women; there I sat in a house well-constructed of oak bark and circular in shape, so that it had the appearance of being built with an arched roof. It contained a great quantity of maize, or Indian corn, and beans of last year's growth, and there lay near the house for drying enough to load three ships, besides what was growing in the fields. On our coming into the house, two mats were spread out to sit upon, and immediately some food was served in well-made red wooden bowls. Two men were also dispatched at once with bows and arrows in quest of game, who soon after brought in a pair of pigeons. They likewise killed a fat dog, and skinned it in great haste with shells they had got out of the water. They proposed that I would remain with them for the night, but I returned, after a short time, on board the ship. The natives are a very good people, for when they saw that I would not remain, they supposed I was afraid of their bows. Taking the arrows, they broke them into pieces and threw them into the fire. Their land is the finest for cultivation that I ever in my life set foot upon. It also abounds in trees of every description.

The following day, adds Juet "the people of the country came flocking alongside, and brought us grapes and pumpkins, which we bought for trifles."

Most important to the subsequent history of this part of North America, these natives would exchange their furs: "Many brought us beaver and otter skins, which we bought for beads, knives and hatchets."

ON 19 SEPTEMBER, above what is now Poughkeepsie, the *Halve-Maen*'s leadsman called out a startling fact—the great "river" they had been slowly ascending was becoming saltless and shallow. Even with its shoal draft, the tiny Dutch vessel could go no farther.

All aboard now realized the *Halve-Maen* must seek some other shortcut to the spices of the Moluccas. Hudson faced downriver from what, in less than five years, would become Fort Orange (later the city of Albany) and the Dutch West Indies Company's most famous trading post in North America. Hudson knew that his substitute discovery of the great river valley would at least permit a dignified return to the company's Amsterdam chambers. Thanks to an insurgent crew, he could now claim for the Netherlands a vast trading area between New France and Virginia never fortified or occupied by other European nations.

But had it been visited before?

A mythical "Castle of Norumbega" (*enorme berge* [Fr.] = massive river banks = "palisades"?) appears on several crude 16th-century large-scale navigational maps of the North American coast, approximating the upriver location of Albany. If Hudson noticed evidence of some undocumented earlier European ascent (or descent?) of the river—rotted remains, perhaps, of a "1540s French fort" on Albany's Castle Island (as one historian vigorously asserted in the 19th century)—the explorer remained discretely silent.

What did it matter if some returning French predecessor had been lost at sea? Hudson himself still had to recross three thousand miles of open, often angry ocean.

From any such thoughts, the captain turned to the fun and games of a godling. En route downriver "our Master determined he would try some of the chief men of the country, whether they had any treachery in them. So he took them down into the cabin, and gave them so much wine and *aqua vitae* [brandy] that they were all merry. In the end, one of them was drunk, and that was strange to them, for they could not tell how to take it. The canoes and folk went all on shore, but some of them came back again and brought strips of beads [wampum] to comfort him. So he slept all night quietly."

The next day "at noon, the people of the country came on board again and saw the savage well, and they were glad. At three o'clock, they brought tobacco and more beads, and gave them to our Master, with an ovation, and brought a great platter of venison, and caused him to eat with them, and make him reverence."

ON 23-24 SEPTEMBER, working down the river at low tide, the *Halve-Maen* twice ran on sandbars, but twice floated free. Near present-day Hudson, New York, a party went ashore and "found good ground for corn and other garden herbs, with great store of goodly oaks, walnut trees, and chestnut trees, and trees of sweet wood in great abundance. And great store of slate for houses."

But the *Halve-Maen*'s crew still faced an emboldened gauntlet of lower river Muhheakunnuk angered by Hudson's earlier abductions. Below them lay the Highlands, the narrowest part of the river. On 1 October came trouble. Juet logged the event.

"This afternoon, one of the canoes, which we could not keep from thence, kept hanging under our stern, with one man in it, who got up by the rudder to the cabin window and stole my pillow, two shirts and two bandoliers." (Hudson had already noted in his own journal: "The natives have a great propensity to steal, and are exceedingly adroit in carrying away whatever they take a fancy to.")

Juet continues: "Our mate shot at him, struck him in the breast and killed him. Whereupon all the rest fled away in their canoes, and also leapt out of them into the water. We manned our boat, and got our things again. Then one of them that swam got hold of our boat, thinking to overturn it. But our cook took a sword and cut off one of his hands, and he was drowned."

The next day, off Croton Point once more "there came one of the savages that swam away from us at our going up the river, with many others, thinking to betray us. Two canoes full of men with bows and arrows shot at our stern. In recompense, we discharged six muskets, and killed two or three of them. Then above a hundred came to a point of land to shoot at us. I shot our small cannon at them and killed two, whereupon the rest fled into the woods. Yet they manned off another canoe with nine or ten men, who came to meet us. So I shot a cannon at it, also, and shot it through and killed one of them. Then our men with their muskets killed three or four more. So they went their way."

AND ON HIS WAY, too, went Henry Hudson, leaving bitter Muhheakunnuk memories swirling like bloodied tides in the great river that would one day bear his name. On 4 October, one month to the day after they entered Lower Bay, Juet tells us, "we weighed our anchor and came out of the river into which we had run so far. . .and continued our course for England. . .and on the seventh day of November, by the grace of God, we arrived safely in Dartmouth."

Two centuries later, Washington Irving would immortalize these first known white men on the Hudson River as sinister wildwood shades with little piggy eyes, "mysteriously silent strangers with. . .long knives in their belts. . .withal the most melancholy party of pleasure Rip had ever witnessed," spawning claps of Catskill thunder from their eternally haunted game of ninepins.

HUDSON'S IMPORTANT DISCOVERY—for the Dutch—was resented by the English, who placed him under genteel house arrest. When the *Halve-Maen* was finally released across the English Channel the following July, the Amsterdam merchants proved far more interested in the market potential of Hudson's furs than in any of the explorer's recorded suggestions for permanent settlement.

Barred from trading with New France and Virginia, the Dutch entrepreneurs and their captains were content to simply sail in and out of their great river for almost a dozen years, exchanging goods at arm's length with the Muhheakunnuk and their hereditary enemies, the Mohawk Nations, mainly for beaver and beaver cods (contemporary male Europeans had developed a curious trust in the prophylactic and restorative powers of dried and powdered beaver testicles). Then, undoubtedly spurred by news that filtered across the Channel of the English establishment of a colony in eastern Massachusetts, the Dutch Estates General approved the formation of the Dutch West India Company with full economic and political responsibility for New Netherlands. But it was not until May of the year 1624 that the first Dutch colonizing ship arrived in Lower Bay, carrying "30 families, mostly Walloons, to plant a true Dutch colony" along both banks of the river Hudson had discovered. The permanent settlement of "Nieuwe Nederlandt" had begun. By then the martyred Hudson had been dead for more than 13 years.

The little settlement slowly grew under a rapid succession of Dutch governors appointed by the Company. The governors' conduct ranged from incompetent to infamous to barbarous. The benchmark of bloodshed between the Dutch and natives in the Hudson Valley, first established by the *Halve-Maen*'s cannon, was perpetuated; settlers immediately attempted (with indifferent success) to subjugate and enslave the natives.

Their Dutch Reformed Biblically ordained racism overrode any possibilities of exotic John Rolfe/Pocahontas relationships; with the exception of a few free-spirited male traders on the frontier or occasional white female captives "gone Indian," native American skin color would provide predictable, adequate excuse for exploitation and legitimatized the inevitable extermination of the aboriginal population.

After less than a generation of contact with steadily increasing numbers of Dutch, most of the Muhheakunnuk rose up in the general rebellion of 1643. Terrible bloodletting marked the beginning of a century-long native struggle for existence.

"Although they were Indians with whom we never had the least trouble," complains an anonymous manuscript in The Hague Royal Library "Pacham, a crafty sachem, had run through all the native villages urging the Indians to a general massacre of the "Swannekens"—the "people from across the salt sea," as the Hudson River natives were soon calling the Dutch traders and settlers. Thereupon it happened that certain Indians called Wappingers, dwelling 16 leagues up the river, seized a boat coming down from Fort Orange, in which were only two men but full 400 beavers. This great booty stimulated others to follow the example, so that they seized two boats more, intending to overhaul the fourth also—from which they were driven with the loss of six Indians. Nine Christians, including two women, were murdered in these captured barks; one woman and two children remaining prisoners. Nothing was now heard but murders."

The fearful Dutch responded in kind. The closest Muhheakunnuk were across the river at nearby Pavonia (Jersey City). An eyewitness relates how "neither age nor sex were spared. Warrior and squaw, sachem and chief, mother and babe were treated alike. Children were taken from the arms of their mothers and butchered, their mangled limbs thrown into the fire or the water. Other sucklings had been fastened to little boards; in this position they were cut to pieces. Some were thrown into the river, and when the parents rushed in to save them, the soldiers prevented their landing and let the parents and children drown."

This brutality inevitably dissolved into escalating madness that made mockery of both Muhheakunnuk and Christian teaching. Before long, an Amsterdam scandal sheet, the *Breeden Raedt* recounted how Dutch immigrant housewives kicked a severed Native American's head like a football up and down Manhattan's Broad Street. In swift native retaliation, hundreds of Muhheakunnuk warriors besieged the Dutch colony farther up the Hudson at Esopus. In full view of the protective stockade, eight Dutch prisoners were stripped naked and tied to stakes circled by a large ring of fire. Their heads were ornamented and their bodies painted. Their nails pulled out, their fingers bitten off or crushed between large stones, their skin scorched with firebrands and torches, pieces of flesh cut from their bodies, and as they died, one by one, their corpses were thrown into the flames.

A long rain of terror fell on both Dutch and natives along the troubled river.

# NOTES

[1]The Dutch East India Company was established in 1602, seven years before Hudson's voyage.
[2]A small open boat with sails, oars, or both.

**Plate 3: Captain Robert Fulton (1765-1815), by Benjamin West (1738-1820).**

# CHAPTER II

# 200 Years Ago: ROBERT FULTON

*Now you will have many visitors from afar that you would never have seen, had not the power of steam been found out.*
—WILLIAM KENNER to Stephen Minor, January 1812

IN THE SAME YEAR, 1765, that Robert Fulton was born, his future business partner Robert R. Livingston graduated from King's [later Columbia] College in New York City. Through their joint financing, construction, and operation of the *North River Steam Boat*—only a later version would be known as the *Clermont*—the names of Fulton and Livingston were inextricably entwined.

ROBERT FULTON, regarded by most Americans as the "inventor of the steamboat," was the fourth child of five born to a Scotch-Irish immigrant tailor and his American wife. The family attempted unsuccessfully to break its bonds of genteel poverty by farming some unpromising land 30 miles south of Lancaster, Pennsylvania. When Robert was seven years old, his father went bankrupt and returned to Lancaster, and tailoring. Lancaster was on its way to becoming a "boom town" of the American Revolution. In 1777, Lancaster actually thrived on the political and economic disruption caused by the British Army's occupation of Philadelphia, 90 miles to the east. When Fulton's father died unexpectedly, his family was left to the charity of relatives.

Growing up in Lancaster, the temporary national capital of the United States, young Fulton encountered an intellectual atmosphere that offered a full rein to his active imagination. At the "open house" maintained by the eclectic scientist and telegraphic experimenter William Henry, the adolescent Fulton, who possessed a quick and inquiring mind, demonstrated an unusual flair for drawing, painting, and the mechanical arts. At a time and in a nation where independence of thought was now prized, Fulton participated fully in discussions with men many years his senior, and was amazed and delighted by Henry's working model of a steam-powered watercraft.

It was clear from the successes of the British-built Newcomen and Watt steam engines in 1711 and 1769 that the coming century would be an age of steam, replacing all traditional methods of land and water transport, commerce, and, quite possibly, warfare.


AT THE AGE OF 15, handsome young Robert Fulton, quite tall for his years, left his home in Lancaster for newly liberated Philadelphia, soon engaging himself as a silversmith's apprentice. It was a time of social ferment in this bustling, sophisticated, wartime metropolis of almost 40,000 people, second city only to London in the English-speaking world. Best of all, despite its sizeable number of leftover royalist sympathizers and disaffected pacifist Quakers, Philadelphia was a city that was now deeply breathing the heady air of independence. The teenaged Fulton, as a nascent artistic and scientific jack-of-all-trades, took every opportunity in the "City of Brotherly Love" to develop profitable new skills.

In quick order he became a miniaturist and a practitioner of the odd and painstaking 18th century art of "hairworking."[1]

Fulton also developed the skills of a more than passable painter of oil portraits and landscapes, working on occasion in the Philadelphia studio and museum of famed artist and showman Charles Willson Peale. Peale himself had studied in wartime London with the superbly gifted American expatriate painter Benjamin West.[2] Although Fulton turned out some creditable work, competition was keen and the wartime cost of art materials in Philadelphia was high. He faced the constant struggle of most young artists of any era—making ends meet.

Then, at the age of 21, plagued again by consumption, Fulton spent almost a year at a fashionable warm spring in the western mountains of Virginia. It was here that he met James Rumsey, chief engineer of a canal then being laid out around the Falls of the Potomac. Rumsey was also working on a boat designed to "walk" upstream against the current and had even considered using steam to propel his mechanism.

When Fulton, fully recovered, returned to Philadelphia, it was only for a brief stay. With borrowed money, he had made up his mind to pursue a career in painting, studying and working in London, a city now 15 times the size of Philadelphia. When he finally sailed eastward across the Atlantic in the spring of 1787—as the framers and politicians at home gathered to debate a new United

States Constitution—Fulton proudly carried a letter of introduction to the ever-generous Benjamin West from Benjamin Franklin.

Before long, Fulton was part of West's huge London entourage and was even welcome in the painter's household. It was the beginning of a warm, candid, and supportive relationship that endured throughout both painters' lives. But for this slightly homesick younger American, his chosen profession proved difficult. Dragging himself out of debt became a tedious and depressing process. In his letters home, Fulton was closemouthed about his new circle of influential friends, which developed after his paintings were finally chosen in 1791 for exhibition at the Royal Academy and London's Society of Artists. By June of that same year, and for the next 18 months, Fulton lived at the elegant Devonshire country seat of 23-year-old Viscount William Courtney.[3]

PORTRAIT COMMISSIONS began to flow from Robert Fulton's new and wealthy circle of friends. His artistic expression slowly gained recognition from the British establishment; the Royal Academy hung four of his paintings in its 1793 exhibition. Three of these paintings dealt with simple historical subjects, including Louis XVI's farewell to his family en route to the guillotine, an event that had just occurred.

On the death of Sir Joshua Reynolds, Benjamin West, a close friend of George III, was elected President of the Royal Academy. Fulton's establishment ties were further enhanced by the marriage of West's son to Fulton's oldest sister, who had been visiting in London. At this point in Fulton's career, a realistic self-appraisal of his many talents was in order. The result was Fulton's renewed interest in mechanical devices, ably supported by his superb drafting skills. He was already responsible for designing improved machinery for carving and polishing decorative slabs of marble.

Fulton's ideas on cheap inland water transport by canal brought the young man to the attention of the no-nonsense Earl of Stanhope. Fulton had developed a scheme, never implemented, that called for a series of lockless canals to serve hilly areas of England with little swift-flowing water.

Stanhope, a wealthy titled entrepreneur who busied himself with improvements in transportation, had in 1790 operated an experimental "steam carriage" on the Continent between Boulogne and Calais. Later on, Stanhope experimented with a model double-ended steam-powered barge, which the leading steam engine designers of the day totally ignored.

Fulton's plans for Stanhope's projected 75-mile canal were ingeniously simple: Small amphibious barges were to be either towed in the canal or moved uphill on built-in wheels. Each barge would be pulled up to a higher section of the canal by the downhill slide of a balancing container that had been slowly filling with water—and subsequently emptied to recycle the process.[4]

The scheme, on which Fulton eventually obtained a patent, signaled the start of a long epistolary and personal relationship between the titled Stanhope and the impecunious mechanical designer. As Fulton immersed himself in the 18th century art of canal-building, he drew away from the Devonshire coterie, replacing those gay friends with new acquaintances from among the British scientific community. His palette and brushes were laid aside for drawing pencils, rulers, and compasses, as he was accepted as a competent and talented, if underemployed, canal engineer.

A result in 1796 was Fulton's handsome 160-page book, with the run-on title, *A Treatise on the Improvement of Canal Navigation, Exhibiting the Numerous Advantages to be Derived from Small Canals, and Boats of Two to Five Feet Wide, Containing from Two to Five Tons Burthen, with a Description of the Machinery for Facilitating Conveyance by Water Through the Most Mountainous Countries, Independent of Locks and Aqueducts, Including Observations on the Great Importance of Water Communications, with Thoughts on and Designs for Aqueducts and Bridges of Iron and Wood.* The author subscribed his name: "R. FULTON, Civil Engineer."

Despite its pretentious title, the book was succinct and modest. Fulton generously acknowledged the earlier work of canal pioneers, loosely subscribing to the theory of scientific discovery and development that may be fairly characterized as "giants standing on the shoulders of pygmies." Two hundred complimentary copies were disseminated where Fulton thought they would do the most good, including a copy to the ex-president of the United States, George Washington, at Mount Vernon. Washington responded favorably.

Things were finally looking up for Fulton. In the spring of 1797, he sold a substantial part of the American construction rights for his small lockless canal scheme to Alexander Hamilton's brother-in-law. In June, Fulton suddenly left London for Paris, ostensibly to secure a French patent on his canal/lock system, before he sailed for America.

WHAT ROBERT FULTON confidently expected would be only a few months stay in Paris turned out to be far longer. At the end of a decade spent mostly in the homes and company of many English friends and benefactors, a tergiversating Fulton had been secretly working on a project devised to help Bonaparte and the French Directory blow the warships of the British Navy—largest fleet in the world—out of the water. Fulton had sketched plans for a three-man muscle-powered military submersible which he called the *Nautilus*.[5]

Fulton's craft was designed to attach a powerful explosive charge, over 200 pounds of gunpowder, under the keel of an anchored British man-of-war.

Little was original in the painter's submarine concept; a quarter century earlier, at the beginning of the American Revolution, a Connecticut farmer-mechanic named David Bushnell had demonstrated a similar craft designed around a single brawny operator. Adapting many of Bushnell's ingenious underwater navigation and life-supporting aids, Fulton's contribution to the art of undersea warfare was primarily one of scale. He also took peculiar comfort in his oft-expressed belief that his success with his submarine would bring a speedy end to any kind of war at sea.

For months, Fulton haggled with the French government over complicated terms for constructing a prototype *Nautilus*, intended to become the cornerstone of a substantial fleet of these early submersibles. Frustrating discussions with the ruling French Directory and Ministry of Marine, despite generally favorable sub-committee reports, stretched on and on. It effectively prevented Fulton's return to the United States, where he had hoped to implement his "small-canal" patent process. Bitter argument raged over the submarine's costs and the special military immunities Fulton had demanded for the crew of his unconventional war vessels. Baffled by his inability to conclude an agreement, the versatile Fulton shifted his energies to additional money-making projects. One attempt was a partnership to develop advanced rope spinning machinery, which was soon dissolved at a financial loss. The other idea was to create a Paris version of the London "skyline," which Fulton helped to paint and house in a special circular building near the Champs Élysees. It was a tremendous success. Lines were long, and it kept Fulton in francs for a critical period.

Fulton's perseverance finally paid off. On 18 Brumaire (November 9) 1799, Napoleon, having recently fled back to France from his disastrous Egyptian campaign, succeeded in overthrowing the Directory, dictatorially establishing himself as France's First Consul. Spurred by a new and Fulton-friendly Minister of Marine, Bonaparte authorized construction and trial of the *Nautilus* in the Seine near the center of Paris.

Borrowing 28,000 francs, Fulton began work on his novel undersea craft, scheduling a demonstration of the completed submarine for June 1800. On the 18th of that month, before a crowd of astonished and delighted Parisians, with Fulton and two associates as crew, the *Nautilus* made twin dives of 15 minutes each. It navigated at some depth in the Seine for a considerable distance before surfacing, raising the "boat-fish's" sail, and tacking upstream against the wind. Fulton finally found himself in the position he had so long coveted—"man of the hour."

Further sea trials of the *Nautilus* followed, downriver to Rouen and at Le Havre, at which time the American was made a temporary admiral in the French Navy—to protect his life from possible British reprisal if his submarine was ever captured. In September, Fulton sailed his vessel up the coast, unsuccessfully seeking to engage the enemy. The following month he laid up the *Nautilus* for the winter.

In the spring of 1801, a long-sought face-to-face discussion took place between Fulton and the Emperor. It ended inconclusively. The "mechanician" (as Fulton now styled himself) continued fruitless maneuvering off the blockaded French Channel ports with both his *Nautilus*, and updated versions of David Bushnell's floating clockwork-mines.[6]

As a second winter neared, Fulton's submarine was taken ashore near Brest, where the hull was now revealed to be no longer seaworthy, incapable of further action the following spring, without extensive and expensive repairs. Fulton's funds were again running low; his vaunted submarine had brought him not a sou of expected prize money. In what now appears to be a fit of pique, he dismantled the *Nautilus*. When Napoleon next inquired about the submarine, he was told that it no longer existed.

But Fulton's submarine had truly captured the imagination of the futurists. In July 1802, the British *Naval Chronicle* soberly reported the observations of a member of the French Marine Tribunal, a M. St. Aubin, that "It is not 20 years since all Europe was astonished at the first ascension of men in balloons. Perhaps in a few years hence they will not be less surprised to see a flotilla of diving boats, which, on a given signal, shall, to avoid the pursuit of an enemy, plunge under water and rise again several leagues from the place where they descended."

IN THE LATE SPRING OF 1802, Robert Fulton, back in Paris again with little to do, finally met a man who would signal a change in his life, while affording him a solid place in the history of transportation as "the inventor of the steamboat." This eminent personage was 56-year-old Robert R. Livingston, scion of an influential, immensely wealthy New York State landowning family on the upper Hudson River. By the end of the Revolution, Livingston's manor spread over 200,000 acres between Massachusetts and the Pennsylvania border. Economic and political rivalries brought the Livingston and Schuyler families into conflict with local and downstate royalists; their choice of Revolutionary sides—and ideologies—was inevitable.

Livingston was a signer of the Declaration of Independence and subsequently became Chancellor of the new State of New York, the state's highest legal office. Livingston had come to Paris as President Jefferson's new Minister to France, in which role he would unexpectedly become involved in the earliest negotiations on the Louisiana Purchase.

An enthusiastic believer in the economic possibilities of steam-driven machinery, Livingston was convinced that the future development of the United States rested, in large part, on the introduction of some form of steam-powered water transport on two major American river systems—the Hudson, discovered by the Dutch soon after the apogee of Spanish world domination, and the Mississippi, widely explored by La Salle 73 years later. The Hudson, a navigable sea-level route, 150 miles between New York City and Albany, was the historic pathway to the continental interior for the Northern and Middle colonies. The Mississippi had always been a frustratingly one-way trade route, carrying the commercial produce of the frontier to market at New Orleans; after their slow thousand-mile voyage downstream, the various river craft that bore the freight were inevitably sold or broken up for their lumber.

It had long been clear to Livingston and a host of other entrepreneurs that the successful operator of a steam power-driven boat capable of traveling up and down both rivers, the Hudson and Mississippi, wholly independent of wind, tide, or current, would quickly become an extremely wealthy man. Many such "inventors"—including Rumsey, Fitch, Stevens, and the Frenchman de Blanc—had grappled with the problem of devising the most efficient method of rapid forward propulsion and had come up with designs that missed. Livingston himself already had at least one expensive failure—a steamboat constructed to his designs in New York by skilled engineer Nicholas Roosevelt, with whom Livingston had signed an 18-year contract.

The supremely self-confident Fulton seemed an unlikely associate for the aristocratic, domineering Livingston. The younger man's canal experiments and minor inventions, most of them now securely under French patents, reflected an extensive knowledge of hydraulics, with its thorny problem of how to best convert mechanical energy into forward motion in an unstable medium—water. Besides his highly developed graphic ability, which always proved useful when explaining his ideas to engineers and laymen alike, Fulton also possessed much of the basic knowledge required to test and build an experimental steamboat—if the new American ambassador could persuade Fulton to drop his preoccupation with man-powered military submersibles.

BY NOW, Fulton was even considering offering the British the same submarine and torpedo (floating mine) designs Bonaparte had slighted. Meanwhile he signed various financial agreements with Livingston and got down to serious, detailed experimentation with a spring-wound model steamboat in a 60-foot-long French test basin. He planned on using a state-of-the-art English-built steam engine for his final full-sized vessel. Fulton's scaled-up empirical calculations projected a slim hull 120 feet long, with only a narrow eight foot beam, to move forward at eight knots. Fulton always insisted that this unique design—which may be compared to a "powered toothpick"—was a major technical breakthrough. If so, it was one that left almost too little space for passengers and cargo.

Complicating his personal situation, Fulton was deeply involved in an outlandish *menage à trois* with Ruth and Joel Barlow; the latter, a well-known American poet and business representative, also served President Jefferson as a minor diplomat in the Mediterranean countries. Ruth Baldwin Barlow's brother, the Georgia Congressman Abraham Baldwin, sent letters allegedly containing comments on the submarine experimentation of David Bushnell, a fellow Yale graduate and a Georgia neighbor of Baldwin's.[7] His invention, the one-man *Turtle* submarine, was used (unsuccessfully) against the Royal Navy in New York Harbor in 1776.

After several false starts, Livingston finally succeeded in capturing Fulton's attentions long enough to convince the younger man that he, Livingston, possessed something apparently no one else had been able to procure, a special Act passed by the Chancellor's cronies in the New York State Legislature. Canceling a privilege previously granted to John Fitch in 1787, the legislators gave the Chancellor a 14-year absolute monopoly on steamboat operation on the Hudson River, provided a successful prototype could be launched and placed in service before 1804, a deadline they extended twice.

Fulton was impressed by Livingston's interests, wealth, and political connections. Before long, the young American expatriate had put his name to a complicated—and in several cases contradictory—series of agreements that would provide the monopolist-manqué with a steam-driven vessel of Fulton's design, to ply the Hudson's waters, thus fulfilling the terms of the State legislation.[8]

FULTON'S FIRST STEP in New York City, now a busy metropolis of more than 100,000 people and the unchallenged gateway to the United States, was to drop a note to Livingston at his luxurious upriver *Clermont* estate, advising him of his eagerness to finally get down to work on their grand moneymaking opportunity. Reunited once more with the Barlows, Fulton joined his friend Joel on a lobbying expedition to the new capital city, Washington, where they surreptitiously examined at least a dozen competing Patent Office applications relating to steamboat configuration and propulsion.

For several months, Fulton busied himself with calculations designed to convince a reluctant Livingston that introducing their first steam vessel to transport merchandise on the Mississippi would provide a higher rate of return on investment than their estimated revenues from freight and passenger service in the Hudson Valley. But Livingston was adamant—first things first—and Fulton finally succumbed, saving face by adjusting his estimates. He began to concentrate at the drawing board, contracting with the experienced East River shipwright Charles Brown to build the hull for the *North River Steam Boat*, as he called it. The new vessel would be far longer than originally anticipated. It would be 146 feet in length and 12 feet wide. The cabin height was sufficient to accommodate a few gentlemen wearing silk top hats. Brown estimated completion of the hull in two months at a cost to the partners of $1,666. Liberating his still uncrated English engine from the warehouse where it had sat for over a year, and settling some U.S. Customs duties his partner had refused to pay, Fulton undertook the supervision of a cadre of skilled shipwrights, engineers, and craftsmen in Brown's boatyard to fabricate the paddle wheel machinery and construct a copper steam boiler. Final cost of the completed vessel was around $5,000, but Fulton and Livingston happily calculated that their monopoly would soon be operating in the black.

In the midst of all the bustle of construction, Fulton was still able to find time to offer to sell his submarine and torpedo plans to the U.S. Secretary of the Navy, who proved uninterested. Nevertheless, as the country's diplomatic relations with Great Britain worsened and impressment of American merchant seamen continued, Fulton put on yet one more explosives demonstration in New York's Upper Bay.

ON 9 AUGUST 1807, four years to the day after his successful demonstration on the Seine, Robert Fulton took his completed steamboat on a trial run from Brown's Corlaers Hook shipyard around Manhattan's Battery and up into the North River, and return.[9] A week later, with a full complement of invited dignitaries, Fulton again steamed around the Battery to his vessel's permanent new berth on the Hudson River near Greenwich Village.

The following day at 1:00 pm, before a crowd of hundreds of excited New Yorkers—including more than a few wags who came to ridicule and confidently wager that "Fulton's Folly" would soon ascend to heaven in an explosive cloud of smoke, steam, and cinders—Fulton cast off from the *North River Steam Boat's* pier, and began moving steadily at 4? knots against wind and tide towards Albany, 150 miles away. Aboard with Fulton were an Engine Operator, a Captain, and a skeleton crew.

TRIUMPHANTLY, the steamboat had come to America.

# NOTES

[1]Use of a sitter's own hair strands to weave a tiny portrait.

[2]West was a peaceable Quaker, the son of a wealthy Philadelphia minister. After a tour of Europe, West had permanently settled in 1763 in London. In 1771, he painted his masterpiece, a huge canvas depicting *The Death of General Wolfe*, before Quebec, thereby creating a new realistic type of subject matter in Western art.
West was the first to break the old taboo of historical painting, as his subjects exchanged the roman toga for military dress.

[3]Courtney's seduction at 16 by the tasteless millionaire art collector William Beckford of Fonthill Abbey had been at the time the gossip of fashionable London.

[4]Fulton's principle was incorporated a century later in a very popular children's gravity seaside toy dubbed "Sandy Andy."

[5]A name immortalized 72 years later by Jules Verne in his fictional masterpiece *Twenty Thousand Leagues Under the Sea*.

[6]Lethal towed mines were first used during the American Revolution by their Connecticut inventor, David Bushnell, against British shipping in the Delaware River (the celebrated "Battle of the Kegs"), and earlier against the Royal Navy near New London on Long Island Sound. Most British officers considered that use of underwater explosives "beastly."

[7]Timothy Dwight, President of Yale, composed a long poem on the rising glory of America in which he eulogized the gifted Bushnell:

> *See Bushnell's, strong, creative genius, fraught*
> *With all th' assembled powers of skilful thought,*
> *His mystic vessel plunge beneath the waves*
> *And glide thro' dark retreats, and coral caves!*

[8]Fulton would prove to be a persevering litigant. In 1812, he was still able to assert his monopoly of all steamship construction and operation in the United States. He wrote President James Monroe, "Sir—I beg you will have the goodness to give a positive order that my patent for steamboats shall not be copied or examined. . .there is nothing in the law authorizing anyone to examine a patent, as it is exclusive and private property for 14 years. . .I have reason to believe that there are persons who desire a copy or copies of my patent to apply my inventions. You will, therefore, I hope, use the power vested in you to prevent any examination of my patent or copies being taken."

[9]So called by the original Dutch colonizers to distinguish it from the "South (Delaware) River," where the Dutch had also planted a settlement.

# CHAPTER III

## *NIEUWE ROTTERDAMSCHE COURANT*
## (New Rotterdam Courant)

New York, Thursday, September 2, 1909

Exclusive Dispatch

### THE HUDSON-FULTON CELEBRATION

FOR SOME TIME NOW, New York City has been preparing for a grand two-week-long celebration on an order of magnitude not seen in this city before. Those responsible for organizing this festivity have received increasing attention from most of the city's otherwise blasé or preoccupied inhabitants.

The planners intend to paint the nighttime city bright with light from thousands of outdoor bulbs and searchlights, which New York has been installing for months. It will also add to the existing illumination of such amusement parks as Dreamland, Luna Park, and others in the city's outlying districts, whose customary light displays during summer nights have always been most impressive. One can also admire the somewhat unsavory "Great White Way," which stretches up from Broadway at Herald Square to Times Square and beyond.

This real sea of electric lights is now being extended by the Hudson-Fulton Celebration Commission to cover most of Manhattan's skyline and waterfront, thereby creating a new "Great White Metropolis."

Several hundred shops are already displaying historic memorabilia of the period, such as different sized replicas of Henry Hudson's *Halve-Maen* and Robert Fulton's *Clermont*; portraits of the two captains;[1] pictures of Dutch windmills; and toy wooden shoes abound, some real, some fake.

It is not surprising to see the names of Hudson and Fulton bandied about left and right in many ordinary public announcements and publications that have little or nothing to do with the Celebration. In this land, advertising plays an important part in people's daily lives. The need to present a product in the best possible light often moves people to buy things they don't need or will rarely use. Americans are the absolute masters in this field. The end results are often eye-catching.

A discernible lack of taste is apparent in the quality of the merchandise offered for sale. The *Halve-Maen*, for example, pictured on colored lithographed postal cards and Delft-Blueware[2] tiles, bears little or no resemblance to the real ship.[3]

In addition, many of the postal cards on sale are labeled "imported," to graft some authenticity to their minimal quality. Most were probably printed in Germany, but the designers apparently had no picture of Henry Hudson's vessel available. As for the New York merchants peddling these items, they probably hope to sell out all this early merchandise before customers could make comparisons with the reconstructed version of the real ship.

As for the Celebration itself, we should first tell a bit about the grand welcome that has been planned for all the celebrants. This includes the local Dutch, both individually and in groups. During the days and nights ahead, they will be occupied with a full and varied schedule. These will include several Dutch dinner parties.

On Saturday, September 18, the "Eendracht Maakt Macht"[4] service organization, established here in New York in 1864, will host a grand dinner. For Tuesday, September 21, the Nederlandsche Club and the Dutch Chamber of Commerce have their own dinner plans. On Wednesday, another major dinner party will be given by the Holland Society and the Knickerbockers, all descendants of the original Dutch colonial settlers of Nieuw Amsterdam.

Yes, one can safely say that the Dutch people here will be extending the kind of warm welcome that only the Dutch can provide.

For all Dutchmen, there will be satisfaction in knowing that the official colors the Hudson-Fulton Commission has chosen for all its decorations are the *oranje-blanje-bleu* of the Dutch flag that once flew atop Hudson's *Halve-Maen* (now with an "H-&-F" monogrammed in the center).

The following is a brief review of the events expected here during the next two weeks:

Saturday, September 25: The main event—Review of the naval vessels and sailing ships, by day and night.

Sunday September 26: Both Hudson and Fulton will be remembered and honored during church services of various denominations.

Monday, September 27: Reception for foreign dignitaries and other honored guests. Opening of special exhibitions and commencement of the aeroplane show.

Tuesday, September 28: Parade with historical theme floats. At night, presentations and speeches at the Metropolitan Opera House, Carnegie Hall, and other auditoriums.

Wednesday, September 29: Water games/sports on the Hudson River.

Thursday, September 30: Armed Forces Parade, including Army, Navy, and National Guard units.

Friday, October 1: *Halve-Maen* and *Clermont* will sail to Newburgh, escorted by a variety of warships, to meet with other vessels coming down from Albany.

Saturday, October 2: A variety of children's activities planned in fifty New York City neighborhoods for approximately 600,000 children. On the Hudson, the flotilla returns from Newburgh. At night a large New York City parade, with many participating organizations, will write *finis* to the formal festivities.

From Sunday to Saturday, October 3-9, a variety of events are planned throughout the Hudson Valley, from Hastings-on-Hudson to Albany. The *Halve-Maen* and *Clermont* will visit each celebrating town.

Sunday, October 10: The historical parade held on Wednesday, September 29, in Manhattan will be repeated in Brooklyn, the Bronx, and Staten Island. In addition, on October 9, there will be a repeat, in Brooklyn, of Manhattan's October 2, historical parade.

Regarding our earlier remarks about the way in which New York City will be lit, one of the Commission members had this to say: "Now that the North Pole has been conquered, and men have learned how to fly, there is only one problem left: how to make day out of night. This will now happen in New York City." In addition to Manhattan's regular street lighting, an extra 1,500,000 electric bulbs will be burning, plus 7,000 arc lights and 8,500 superannuated gas lights. A battery of 17 searchlights, each with the power of 100,000 candles (all together 1,700,000 candles) will illuminate the events on the river. Add to all this the hundreds of thousands of lights from stores, advertising signs, private residences, and so forth.

Riverside Park between 72nd and 130th Streets—the center of most activities—will bask in a sea of light. On the New Jersey side of the Hudson, plans are under way to equal New York's lighting spectacle. Of special interest will be the illumination of the three bridges across the East River (two of them newly built) from Manhattan to Long Island. About 37,000 more lights will be used for this purpose. A number of structures will also be spotlighted, such as City Hall, the Memorial Arch at Washington Square, and General Ulysses S. Grant's tomb. The entire route of the parades will be illuminated with strings of light.

A number of huge torches, each 30 feet high, will be ignited between Staten Island and Albany to mark the close of this grand illuminated Celebration.

This initial report, setting forth our introduction to such an unusual international gathering has gone on a bit longer than intended, but there is so much to tell. More next week about the continuing preparations.

EXTRACT FROM THE OFFICIAL NEW YORK STATE HISTORY (1910)
OF THE HUDSON-FULTON CELEBRATION:

[THE OFFICIAL International Invitation was printed on handmade paper.]

The Hudson-Fulton Celebration Commission of The State of New York has the honor to invite [NAME OF GUEST] to attend the Tercentenary Celebration of the discovery of the Hudson River by Henry Hudson in 1609, and the centenary of its first successful navigation by steam by Robert Fulton in 1807. To be celebrated in New York from September 25th to October 9th, 1909.
    (signed) General Stewart L. Woodford, Joseph H. Choate, Henry W. Sackett.

At the first meeting of the original Hudson Tercentenary Joint Committee held December 16, 1905, three distinct aims were put forth as worthy of serious attention: First, that a permanent memorial should remain after the Celebration; second, that a naval parade should be one of the prominent features; third, that the keynote of the festivities should be marine in nature, commanding all the resources of the Hudson River and its valley.

THE PLAN submitted in June 1906 contemplated a celebration extending over a period of two weeks. It was believed at first that the larger naval vessels could go only as far upstream as Haverstraw Bay, but it was recommended that the replicas of the *Halve-Maen* and *Clermont* with an escort fleet would proceed up the river as far as Albany, stopping by major riverside villages and cities en route, and forming the center of local demonstrations. In the weeks and months to come, it was made plain that some of the naval vessels could navigate only as far as Newburgh, and the plan was modified accordingly. The plan also provided for commemorative exercises in all the universities, colleges, and institutions of learning throughout the state.

AMONG THE ACTIVE PREPARATIONS during the year before the Celebration, none involved objects of greater popular interest than the building of the replicas of Hudson's ship, the *Halve-Maen* and Fulton's steamboat, the *Clermont*. On December 16, 1905, the first official meeting of the Executive Committee of the Hudson Tercentenary Commission, decided that a facsimile of the *Halve-Maen* be built in Holland if possible, and that it should arrive in New York Harbor and in due time proceed up the Hudson River to Albany, duplicating local anchorages of the original vessel, with celebrations along the way. Research was conducted in Dutch museums and libraries with a view toward preparing authentic data for reconstructing the vessel as a gift from the people of Holland to the people of New York.
    No contemporary image of the ship was known to exist. However, an analysis of Hudson's first mate's log provided sufficient data to determine the *Halve-Maen*'s masting, rigging, draft, and other details. Her tonnage was ascertained

Plate 4:  Launching of the *Half-Moon* replica at Amsterdam.
Plate 5:  Stern view of the *Half-Moon*.

**Plate 6: Lowering the *Half-Moon* from the *Soestdijk*,
Brooklyn Navy Yard, 23 July 1909.
Plate 7: The *Half-Moon* in New York Harbor.**

from archives of the Dutch East India Company. Reference was also made to old maps whose vignettes reflected the exterior appearance of similar vessels. Further research uncovered a complete set of 16th-century plans of the *Halve-Maen*'s sister ship *Hope*. It had been rigged, fitted, and cost the same as the *Halve-Maen*. Reference was also made to a 1606 engraving of Amsterdam's waterfront, showing many different types of vessels, including the type of the *Halve-Maen*. To all this data was added a previously unknown private collection of early Dutch ship models. Plans for the construction were confirmed by United States Navy architects under Admiral Joseph B. Coghlan, and shipbuilding began during the fall of 1908 at the Royal Shipyards in Amsterdam.

The Dutch government gave the Committee several great balks of oak timber which had lain submerged in the wet dock at the yard for over a hundred years. Without too much time to spare, the keel was laid in October 1908, and the ship was launched in April 1909—probably a construction record. She was taken by water to Rotterdam and there hoisted aboard the Holland-America Line steamship *Soestdyk*. Arriving in New York July 22, 1909 she was brought to the Brooklyn Navy Yard, where the *Halve-Maen*, 58 feet long by 16 feet wide, was lifted from her cradle on deck and deposited in the water.

A few days before the Celebration opened, the Dutch cruiser *Utrecht* arrived in New York Harbor and supplied the 20-man crew for the *Halve-Maen*, under Lieutenant Commander William Lam, who would portray Henry Hudson. His sailors were dressed in costumes of the period of Hudson's voyage.


BUILDING THE REPLICA of Robert Fulton's pioneer steam-powered vessel, the *Clermont* (originally called the "North River Steamboat"), came next in the Commission's planning. It is a curious fact that the Naval Parade Committee had greater difficulty determining the appearance of the *Clermont*, which was built in 1807, than in determining the appearance of Henry Hudson's *Halve-Maen*, which entered the river in 1609. Not only did the Committee lack contemporary pictures of the *Clermont*, but authentic descriptions of its details were also lacking. Since the *Clermont* was a pioneer vessel, not much help could be drawn from the appearance of other ships of that period.

Based on Fulton's private letters, the Committee at length arrived at the conclusion that the original *Clermont* was 150 feet long and 13 feet wide and drew only two feet of water. The keel was laid down in the yards of the Staten Island Shipbuilding Company. Observing temperance sensibilities, the vessel was launched on July 10, 1909, by breaking an ornate bottle of upstate spring water over her bow, in place of the customary champagne. Another colorful aspect of the launch was the release of a dozen carrier pigeons from a basket on the bow of the boat. One of the birds covered the ten miles from Staten Island to its rooftop coop on Manhattan's West 11th Street in 15 minutes.

The new *Clermont* was soon moored in the Kill van Kull awaiting the great Naval Parade on September 25. Almost wall-sided and painted a drab gray, she was a quaint-looking craft, in the midst of a fleet of gigantic modern steamships and warships.

**Plate 8: Launching of the *Clermont* (the "North River Steamboat") at New York City.**

# NOTES

[1]There is no contemporary likeness of Hudson, only an illustrator's fancy; Fulton, on the other hand, painted several excellent self-portraits.

[2]Distinctively styled, very popular blue-and-white glazed faience (earthenware) pottery, manufactured since the 16th century in the Dutch city of Delft.

[3]The "real" ship had been reconstructed in Holland and freightered across the Atlantic as a celebratory gift from the Dutch people to the citizens of New York City. The design was based on an old set of plans for a similar vessel.

[4]The Dutch fraternal organization, "In Union There is Strength."

# CHAPTER IV

## *NIEUWE ROTTERDAMSCHE COURANT*

New York, Sunday, September 12, 1909

Exclusive Dispatch

### THE HUDSON-FULTON CELEBRATION

AS IT DRAWS NEAR, one gets a better sense of all the hours, days, and even years that have gone into planning this unusual international celebration. Shops are being decorated and one can expect that *oranje-blanje-bleu* will be the combination of colors most often displayed in New York during the next few weeks.

In a proclamation issued yesterday, Mayor George B. McClellan[1] asked the citizens of New York to fly the Dutch flag (under which the *Halve-Maen* sailed) next to the Star Spangled Banner. The Dutch *Utrecht*, first of a number of warships to arrive in New York Harbor, lent an undeniable naval presence to the proceedings.[2]

When it sailed up the Hudson River, the cruiser immediately became the target for press photographers, and its picture was constantly featured in many of the New York newspapers. In addition, some of the papers contained a picture of the *Utrecht's* commander, Lieutenant Colonel G. P. van Hecking-Colenbrander, along with Lieutenant Commander William Lam, and Lieutenant De Meester. A complement of 20 sailors from the *Utrecht* dressed in old Dutch sailing costumes will man the *Halve-Maen*. Commander Lam is playing the role of Henry Hudson, as Lieutenant A. de Bruijne enacts the part of Hudson's boatswain Robert Juet.

Earlier, as most of the invited guests from Holland were still trooping aboard the liner *Nieuw Amsterdam* at Rotterdam for their voyage here, the special German envoy Admiral Hans Ludwig Raimund von Koester began his own New York trip aboard the German warship *Blücher*. He will be in command of his country's squadron in the upcoming naval event. In Washington, however, there still is no agreement over whether Admiral von Koester or British Admiral Sir Edward Seymour will be the top-ranking guest of honor at both the official reception and the dinner which is being hosted by the United States. A handful of the sensational newspapers have already written about a "possible war between England and Germany over the proper Hudson-Fulton protocol." Others have suggested that a simpler solution may be found, with no need to bring the matter before the International Court of Arbitration in The Hague.

An important event of the coming festivities will be an exhibition of Dutch art. We also think that the naval show, at least from an artistic point of view, should not be underestimated. Indeed, it promises to be an awesome display—53 warships from the United States, a German squadron, four British vessels, and so forth.

At night the illuminated ships, the crisscrossing searchlights, and all the other kinds of illumination on the river should create a most picturesque effect.

A commemorative bronze medal, designed by the Austro-British sculptor Emil Fuchs, has been minted in honor of the celebration. The face of the coin depicts the discovery of the Hudson River by Henry Hudson. The rim of the coin reads, "Discovery of Hudson River by Henry Hudson, A.D. MDCIX. Hudson-Fulton Celebration comm. The American Numismatic Society." The bottom of the design shows Hudson's ship, with the words, "Halve" and "Maene" on either side. The reverse of the medal depicts an allegorical display of Robert Fulton's work, crowned by his bust. More than 80,000 copies of this medal have already been struck. A few minted in gold will be presented to the reigning Heads of State whose warships represent them here. Members of the Committee and their official guests will receive the same medal in silver.

**Plate 9: Official Hudson-Fulton Celebration Medal.**

EXTRACT FROM THE OFFICIAL NEW YORK STATE HISTORY (1910)
OF THE HUDSON-FULTON CELEBRATION:

FOR THE MEDALLIC ARTWORK, "Heinrich" was replaced by "Henry," on the evidence that Captain Hudson was an Englishman, and his name was written "Henry" three times in his contract with the Dutch East India Company. It was similarly signed to that paper, notwithstanding the fact that the contract was prepared by a Dutch lawyer, written in the Dutch language, and executed in Amsterdam.

THE PROPER SPELLING of the name of the vessel was not so readily determined. Publications of Holland spelled the name *Halve-Maen*. Having a high naval authority for this spelling of the ship's name, the medal dies were prepared accordingly. In the end, the Commission learned that no names at all appeared on ship transoms or bows of that era.

In the case of Henry Hudson himself, it was also concluded that no authentic portrait of Hudson existed in 1909, or earlier. While it would have been easy to appropriate some type of an English seadog of that date, for an imaginative 1909 representation, it was thought best in the interest of a permanent historical record, as such a medal must be, not to introduce into the design anything that required the explanation that it really was not what it pretended to be.

There were similar difficulties in accurately representing the shape of the *Clermont*. The best evidence was obtained from a picture of the Port of New York 100 years ago. An important print from that period was used in the design of the *Clermont* medal.

The Clermont Committee had difficulty determining the appearance of the mechanical details of the final *Clermont*. Research among old records brought to light unexpected information, for several changes were made in the location of the paddle wheel, the flywheel, the smokestack, and in the number of masts in her rigging. The design of the medal, even after being delivered to the diemakers, was twice altered. Under the circumstances, this should hardly be surprising.

# NOTES

[1]Son of the famous Civil War Union general.

[2]H.M.S. *Utrecht* was one of six powerful state-of-the-art "*Holland*-class" twin-screw cruisers laid down in 1897 to strengthen the Dutch Navy against any potential European/colonial conflicts. Each warship was longer than a football field and heavily armed and armored.

# CHAPTER V

## *NIEUWE ROTTERDAMSCHE COURANT*

New York, Sunday, September 19, 1909

Exclusive Dispatch

### THE HUDSON-FULTON CELEBRATION

AFTER ALMOST 150 YEARS, New York is once again "Nieuw Amsterdam," and firmly in the grip of the Dutch. This peaceful 1909 reconquest promises to be almost as glorious as the days of 17th-century Dutch exploration and colonization.

But the Dutch surrender of New Amsterdam to the English in 1664 is today still a bit incomplete; the New York State banner, whose orange-white-blue panels are directly derived from the Dutch flag, currently waves over every important facade in town.

It is not only with flags and bunting that this event is being celebrated. There are also the two romantic centerpieces; the Dutch-built full-sized replica of the explorer's tiny *Halve-Maen* and Fulton's *Clermont*. They offer a striking symbol of early ocean and inland navigation, discovery, and settlement. The re-created ships contribute so much more to the celebrants' sense of history. No one ever dreamed that the "younger" edition of Henry Hudson's little vessel would be so important to the success of all the festivities; Americans seem enormously pleased.

A highly visible sign of the Dutch influence here is the place of honor given to the Dutch heavy cruiser *Utrecht*. As a special favor, the Dutch warship was allowed to berth at the Brooklyn Navy Yard in Wallabout Bay, across the East River from Manhattan. Both the *Utrecht* and the little *Halve-Maen*, particularly the latter, hold thousands of Americans enthralled, day in and day out. There is even a need to protect the *Halve-Maen* from souvenir-hunting Yankees. As Colonel van Hecking-Colenbrander, commanding the *Utrecht*, told this correspondent, it was Colonel W. D. H. Baron van Asbeck, Commander of the cruiser *Gelderland*, who, during a planning visit to New York in 1907, first conceived of building the *Halve-Maen* replica as a present to the people of the City of New York from the Dutch. Although others may have come up with the same idea, many friends of the present head of the Royal Naval Institute in Niewdiep would like to credit Colonel van Asbeck for his foresight in reconstructing the *Halve-Maen*.

AS IF TAKEN BY STORM, New York has now surrendered the city to the Dutch Hudson-Fulton Commission, with Mr. J. T. Cremer as special chief representative of the Dutch Government. All information about the participation of the various local Dutch service organizations has been eagerly gobbled up by the New York press. One newspaper has carried photographs of Dutch Lieutenant William Lam and Midshipman 1st Class de Meester with an extensive front page story about last night's highly successful Henry Hudson memorial dinner party. The event was hosted by the Dutch service organization E.M.M.

Attending the dinner were representatives from such organizations as the Netherlands Chamber of Commerce, the Netherlands Charitable Society, the Dutch Committee for the Hudson-Fulton Celebration, the New Netherlands division of the Algemeen Nederlandsche Verbond, the Dutch Club of New York, and so forth. Dutch Consul General J.R. Planten, an honorary member of E.M.M., offered the first dinner toast, to Her Majesty Queen Wilhelmina. He warmly recalled how the recent blessed event in the Royal household solidified the outlook for the future of the Netherlands.[1] Consul Planten also alluded to the unbreakable tie between all Dutchmen dwelling in foreign countries.

Colonel van Hecking-Colenbrander, commanding the *Utrecht*, spoke of the advantages of having a strong navy, from a historical and present-day point of view. He noted that the Dutch tricolor is again flying from a Dutch warship in the second most important port city in the world, even though he himself would have preferred to see an entire naval squadron—as large as the one The Hague recently ordered to the Far East.

This dignified representative of a group of Dutch seafarers was well-liked by leading New Yorkers. The Colonel eloquently expressed the regret of many naval officers that their wives could not also be present at the dinner party. With many endearing words of praise for the beautiful sex, he invited the members of the E.M.M. organization and their spouses to view the forthcoming naval show from the decks of the *Utrecht*.

Other speeches followed, including one by the eloquent president of the E.M.M., Mr. W. van der Hoeven. He spoke about the positive things that could flow from all kinds of Dutch-American organizations getting together. He certainly can boast of his own group (formed in 1864), which, under his effective leadership, has entered a new era of growth.

Adding to the festive mood was a Dutch marching band with a collection of folk songs orchestrated for the occasion by the E.M.M., as well as a table full of simple old Dutch dishes, such as fresh shellfish, renowned since the days of Henry Hudson, *oranje-blanje-bleu* soup, Dutch sole, old Dutch style potatoes, Queen Wilhelmina turkey, Nassau *oranje* cakes, New World ice cream, cakes and other pastries, Java coffee, cigars from Sumatra, and cigarettes from the West Indies.

It was truly a banquet to remember.

---

EXTRACT FROM THE OFFICIAL NEW YORK STATE HISTORY (1910)
OF THE HUDSON-FULTON CELEBRATION:

DR. JOKICHI TAKAMINE, representing his government and the Japanese residents of New York City, brought a goodwill offering from Japan of 2,100 cherry trees to be planted in the park along Riverside Drive. "What the cherry tree is to Japan," Dr. Takamine said, "we would wish it to symbolize to you—the ever-living spirit of the land, bringing with every spring a world of blossom and joy. May this river of blooms flow year after year as a flowering witness to all time of the Japanese affection for New York and the United States of America."[2]

# NOTES

[1]In April, Queen Wilhelmina (1886-1962) of the Royal House of Orange had given birth to Princess Juliana, in whose favor she abdicated 39 years later.

[2]After almost a century, the cherry trees still bloom every spring along Riverside Drive.

# CHAPTER VI

## *NIEUWE ROTTERDAMSCHE COURANT*

New York, Sunday, September 20, 1909

Exclusive Dispatch

THE WEATHER FORECAST this morning was for a day of cloudy skies and an occasional rain shower. Although the New York heavens remained gray for almost the entire day with some patches of fog, only a few drops of rain were felt.

However, when the liner *Nieuw Amsterdam* finally sailed into the harbor, the fog suddenly lifted and rays of sunshine pierced through the clouds. As a result, the Dutch travelers aboard the steamship were able to fully appreciate the majestic beauty of Lower Bay, New York Harbor, and the Hudson River.

Mr. Adrian Gips of the Holland-America Line and Mr. G. Wager Fry of the Hudson-Fulton Celebration Commission went out in a fast launch to greet the important guests.

A number of New York newspapers were represented by their reporters and photographers, and the midday editions showed deckside pictures of Mr. and Mrs. J. T. Cremer, Mr. J. P. van Eeghen and Mr. W. F. van Leeuwen, Mayor of Amsterdam. The New York *Globe*, with amazing technical speed, was able to print a picture of the entire party together with the captain of the *Nieuw Amsterdam*, taken en route to the pier. Some of the newspapers carried such headlines as, "DUTCH RE-TAKE NEW AMSTERDAM WITHOUT FIRING A SHOT."

To the press, Mr. van Leeuwen spoke enthusiastically of his first impressions of New York: the wooded hills of Staten Island, the green shoreline of Brooklyn, and finally the closely spaced tall buildings of Lower Manhattan, with the Singer Building and Metropolitan Life tower rising above all others. He mentioned that America had learned a lot from the Dutch in the past, but those roles now seem to have been reversed. "You are a young nation," Mr. van Leeuwen said, "but you know that a father can sometimes learn much from a clever son." The Dutch mayor also mentioned that no matter how impressive New York's colossal buildings and bridges are, he hoped that this American style would not find its way to Holland. "I love the picturesque," said Mr. van Leeuwen to a reporter from the *Evening Post*, "But Holland is far more picturesque than New York. Here everything is business." According to Mr. van Leeuwen, "In Amsterdam, we are hustlers too, but our ways are evidently different from yours."

The *Evening Post* praised Mr. Cremer as one of the first entrepreneurs to help Dutch-owned Sumatra become an important tobacco supplier, thereby making it of great importance to Holland.

Many Americans seemed astonished to hear all the members of the Dutch committee speaking fluent English, even though most of them had not been to the United States before. The guests are staying at the stately Plaza Hotel, with its beautiful view of the magnificent Central Park.

On Tuesday, the guests will inspect the *Halve-Maen*, while on Wednesday they will be attending a dinner party at the Hollandsche Club. The next few days will be busy.

It would not be fair to ignore the Dutch sailors, after having spent more than a few words on the official Dutch representatives. Coney Island, one of the great unnatural wonders of the New World is a major attraction for our sailors and on a number of occasions we saw them inquire about how to get there by underground transport. In addition, the public seems to think that German is the language of the Dutch. Our sailors are often addressed in German, which is usually not understood. As an example, we noticed today how some sailors were given directions to the New York office of the *Staats-Zeitung*, a German-language newspaper. The person addressed apparently thought that the sailors would find some countrymen there. We hope Mr. Herman Ridder, the newspaper's publisher, who probably feels Dutch enough these days, was not too inconvenienced.

There seems to be a boundless need for Americans to gather souvenirs, and in crowded situations, Dutch sailors may lose their hats to souvenir hunters. So the *Halve-Maen* must be carefully guarded at all times in order to prevent visitors from making off with pieces of her sails. But the worst thing happened to Prince Kuniyoshi Kuni, Japan's official ambassador to the Celebration. As he left the reviewing stand in Riverside Park, from whence he had viewed the parade of ships, a crowd closed in on him. Because of his small stature, the Prince was easily swallowed up. First he lost his black silk top hat, then some buttons ripped off his coat. He was finally saved by two burly policemen who lifted the terrified Prince, his arms stiffly akimbo, high above the shoving crowd and carried him away, while other policemen had to use their nightsticks to clear a path. Charles Evans Hughes, Governor of New York State, later apologized to the Prince for the treatment he received and blamed the police for their lack of crowd control.

It is not surprising that some officers of the British fleet got into a fight with the New York press, who apparently attempted to get permission to board the British flagship *Inflexible*, but were discourteously waved off. The incident was unusual since the British press in all its reporting has seemed to suggest that the Hudson-Fulton festivities are a British-American affair. Of course, New Yorkers do not believe this, and since the New York press has either a perceived or real bone to pick with the British guests, this carefully propagated fiction will most likely not be maintained much longer, even in London.

---

EXTRACT FROM THE OFFICIAL NEW YORK STATE HISTORY (1910)
OF THE HUDSON-FULTON CELEBRATION:

NEW YORK CITY was a perfect place for a world gathering, not only because of its geographic features and natural resources, but its many types of mass transit: surface trolley cars, elevated railways, and underground subways all facilitated the handling of great crowds. In addition, New York lay between two rivers and was easily reached by boat or rail.

A FEW DAYS prior to the official beginning of the Hudson-Fulton Celebration, the Metropolitan Museum of Art opened a remarkable exhibition of Old Master Dutch paintings. They included works previously donated to the museum by its current President, Pierpont Morgan, with additional loans from the financier's private art collection. On display were more than one hundred paintings and drawings by artists of Henry Hudson's period: Rembrandt, Hals, Cuyp, Ruisdael, Vermeer, and others. There were also examples of furniture, silver, pewter, pottery, and glass crafted from about 1625 to 1815, the year of Fulton's death. All the art on display was vetted by Morgan curator, Miss Belle da Costa.

# CHAPTER VII

## *NIEUWE ROTTERDAMSCHE COURANT*

New York, Sunday, September 22, 1909

Exclusive Dispatch

### THE HUDSON-FULTON CELEBRATION

IT HAS BEEN RAINING ALL MORNING, giving New York a gray and dreary look. Above the rivers and the harbor lay what felt like a thick wet blanket. The sonorous growls of foghorns alternated with shriller warning whistles, made the day's outlook even more melancholy. Small craft that earlier had joyously sallied forth to greet the Celebration's arriving warships came about off Sandy Hook and dejectedly slunk back to the city's wharves. In this unhappy weather, everything wore a dismal appearance.

Yesterday, under a clear blue sky that heralded the arrival in the city of Dr. Frederick Cook,[1] the identical whistles had made everyone jump for joy. Today, disappointed people could only walk the streets, listening to the continuous deep lamentations of the foghorns.

On a beautiful day, so many flags and decorations would make the blood rush through your veins. But how sad one feels when those same flags droop disconsolately under the weight of the soaking rain.

You hardly notice the handsome facades of the buildings on Wall and Broad Streets. The weather overwhelms everything. New York was like that almost the entire day.

Then, all of a sudden, about four o'clock, the skies cleared, the sun came out, and the popular mood changed abruptly. Shopkeepers in every corner of the city came rushing out with their flags and other decorations.[2] In minutes, they were busily hanging the *oranje-blanje-bleu* colors in graceful pleats. People paused briefly on Broad Street in front of the five-year-old Stock Exchange building, to stare approvingly as the first flag decorations were being placed in the center of the visitors' gallery. They are our princely colors, with the orange and blue a bit darker-tinted than what we have seen earlier throughout the city. The results are more vivid and historically correct. One can also look at the Drexel building, the home of J.P. Morgan & Co., which also is decorated in good taste. Across the street is the U.S. Sub-Treasury building with its stately steps and the statue of George Washington at the top. Following U.S. tradition, only the Star Spangled Banner can wave over the federal building.

As the grayish damp clouds cleared away, one notices how the decorations on William Street made its dirty-looking houses stand out even more.

We now approach a bunch of street vendors who in their own vernacular "peddle" their Hudson-Fulton medallions, neckties, programs, maps, and much more. We pass them by, knowing that here in this town where you put coins in vending machines without getting anything in return, where you buy Hudson-Fulton souvenir books that are void of any reference to either Hudson or Fulton, where there are so many fakers and fakes that might as well be called fraudulent, it is here that you have to be careful what you buy on the street. In the end, we are so afraid to be tricked that even the people in orange-white-blue hats are not to be trusted with our dime for a program guide to the festivities, touted as "official."

There is colorful activity indeed, as New York dresses up for the great celebration. Everything is coming together at the same time: the Hudson-Fulton festivities, the Cook and Peary hullabaloo, and an important local election.[3]

People seem to be so interested in what is coming, that they can easily lose track of what is already here. That a few citizens were nearly killed yesterday in the first pre-election riot was hardly mentioned by the press. The papers did, however, give space to a story that the Parks Commissioner decided to dismantle an already assembled grandstand near Central Park South, because graft was involved in its placement for prime viewing. But it is not long before that episode is completely forgotten. On the street or in office building elevators, you hear one moment from Cook supporters that their hero is all right and Peary is a faker, and the next moment you hear just the opposite from a Peary adherent. And immediately thereafter, it is back to other events of the day.

In Lewes, Delaware, today, people are celebrating the 300th anniversary of Hudson's discovery of Delaware Bay and River. They are also commemorating the establishment of the first Dutch colony in North America by David Pietersen de Vries. Several years ago, Judge George Bray of Wilmington unveiled a stone memorial at the Lewes site where de Vries erected his Dutch settlement. At that time, a speech in which the Judge gave high praise to Holland was answered in kind by our envoy to Washington, Junker Loudon.  Lewes is also reported to be handsomely decorated in mostly Dutch colors. The United States government is officially represented at Lewes by a battleship, and six torpedo boats. Tomorrow the festivities in Lewes will be history, but those people who cannot get enough of the celebration will move on to New York, where the real party is about to begin.

We have a list of all the ships that will soon be parading on the magnificent stage of the Hudson River: Four German warships under Grand Admiral von Koster; four British warships under Fleet Admiral Sir Edward Seymour; three French warships under Rear Admiral Le Pord; the Italian training vessel *Aetna* in addition to a third class cruiser; the Dutch warship *Utrecht*—already in New York Harbor; Mexico's gunboat *Bravo*; the Cuban *Hatney*; and the Argentine training vessel *Presidente Sarmiento*.

Russia is represented by its naval attache in Washington, Captain Vassiliev; Japan did not send any warships but is represented in New York by Prince and Princess Kuniyoshi Kuni, members of the royal family. And the United States is participating in the festivities with sixteen battleships, three armored cruisers, three reconnaissance cruisers, and a dozen torpedo boats, not to mention submarines and all sorts of smaller craft—fifty-three vessels in all. A goodly naval presence indeed, clearly marking the seagoing character of the entire celebration.

It is whispered that the floats participating in the on-land portion of the pageants will be manned by people who do not speak a word of either Dutch or French, despite the fact that the floats depict scenes from both Dutch and Huguenot time periods. Even so, the great show is almost ready to begin.

---

EXTRACT FROM THE OFFICIAL NEW YORK STATE HISTORY (1910)
OF THE HUDSON-FULTON CELEBRATION:

A BIT OF LATER HISTORY

In 1631, the Dutch West Indies Company dispatched David de Vries and 28 men to a spot on the eastern shore of Delaware Bay, opposite Cape May. Here they created a settlement which they named *Zwandael*. It was the organized beginning of "New Netherlands" in the New World. At the same time, they named the lower reaches of the Delaware River the "South River" to distinguish it from the Hudson, which slowly thereafter became known as the "North River." Although the little Dutch colony on Delaware Bay was extinguished by rival English claims and Native American raids, it existed long enough for the colony of Delaware to use its initial boundary lines to break away a number of southern counties from Maryland to form the new colony—and State—of Delaware.

AFTER THE 77,000 copies of the Celebration poster were distributed, hundreds of requests for more posters were received from schools, colleges, libraries, etc. But because of the cost and difficulties of distribution, no further posters were made available. Their absence made the appearance of a commemorative two-cent postage stamp doubly welcome. At the post office department in Washington, this stamp was regarded as one of the most artistic ever issued by the United States government. Fifty million of them were printed. Sales began on the Celebration's opening day in New York City, and the stamps were soon available at post offices throughout the nation.

---

## From the *COURANT*'s Foreign News Desk

From Lewes, Delaware, Reuters also cabled us today as follows:

The 300th anniversary of Henry Hudson's discovery of the Delaware River was celebrated here today. The Dutch Ambassador to the United States was the guest of honor.

Reuters has sent us an elaborate description of this initial part of the Hudson-Fulton Celebration, as well as details of the program. We will only share with you some of the information hitherto unavailable to our readers. What Reuters communicates about the meaning of the Celebration should, in our opinion, be ignored, because the news agency suggests that "the Celebrations are specifically held to honor both the English and the Dutch," something which in our minds, at least, is highly exaggerated.

In Great Britain one reads, of course, about "the repeated glorification of England" by the citizens of the United States, who "consider English as the Mother tongue" and who "do not easily forget the special assistance Great Britain gave to the United States during the late Spanish-American War."

One fact that may also be noted is the marked absence of President Taft, who had already committed himself to visit the exhibition in Seattle.[4]

# From the Wilmington *Evening Journal*
## September 22, 1909

Lewes had the biggest day in its long history today, when, with imposing ceremony and a parade nearly two miles in length, the new de Vries Monument was unveiled at the point where the first Dutch explorers landed.

The Celebration commemorates the 300th anniversary of the arrival of Henry Hudson, August 28, 1609, and the arrival of the colony sent out by David de Vries in April 1631. The colonists came under a charter of the West Indies Company. They were 28 in number and engaged in whaling and farming.

The minister from the Netherlands to the United States, Baron Jonkheer Loudon, was the guest of honor, and arrived at the celebration in a special car attached to the regular train, which was about forty minutes late. He was escorted to Lewes by a distinguished delegation of representative men.

The area was a part of New Netherlands in America until June 1681, when it became part of New York Colony, and later was surrendered to Pennsylvania, and finally to Delaware when that colony was erected out of Maryland's southern counties. When today's official party arrived at Lewes, they found the First Delaware Infantry drawn up in line to receive their distinguished guests. Among the most beautiful floats in the parade to the monument was one depicting the throne room of the Dutch Queen, surrounded by the ladies of her court. Other floats represented the early Dutch settlers, their homes, churches, and forts.

By now a drizzling rain had commenced and the ceremonies went forward quickly. The huge American flag draping the stone was removed as the showers resolved themselves into a hot mist, even more uncomfortable.

Baron Loudon then apologized, "I am only sorry that I was unable to get you the *Halve-Maen* from New York," he said. "I understand they will be seeking a place for it after the celebration. On Hudson's way to find a new passage to the East Indies he stopped here, in this Bay, but soon found that the river was not the outlet he sought. He stopped here, probably, because he wanted to get a drink. I don't think, strong drink. We Dutch are most quaint and democratic, but we have a Queen whom we adore. It is the most pleasant sight to see my Queen represented by one of the most lovely ladies I ever saw. I was told on the train, when passing New Castle, that the best products of that city are the prettiest girls in the country, but since I have seen the Queen in Lewes, I believe Lewes is the place.

I thank you for listening to me and I will not fail to tell my Queen and the government of this occasion."

## From the Wilmington *Morning News*
### September 22, 1909

Baron Jonkheer Loudon, the minister to the United States from Holland, arrived in this city at 6:10 o'clock last evening, and was met at the Pennsylvania Railroad station by local dignitaries. The Baron was escorted to the home of Henry B.Thompson, where the Ambassador was the guest of honor at dinner. This morning he is accompanying the general committee to Lewes with a party who will be leaving on the regular down train at 8:36 o'clock. The city's organized militia will leave Wilmington on another train at 6:40 am., and the New Castle, Newark, Dover, and Milford companies will board the Lewes train en route.

The parade at Lewes will be interesting and imposing. Heading the procession will be Governor Simeon S. Pennewill and his staff. The parade will form on King Street near the railroad station.

Offshore, the United States has sent the battleship *Montana* with the Atlantic Squadron of torpedo boats and destroyers. It will be a big day in Lewes, when the de Vries monument will be unveiled with befitting ceremonies. The Delaware Railroad Company will run special excursion trains to Lewes.

# NOTES

[1] The contentious, persecuted American Polar explorer.

[2] The New York Hudson-Fulton Committee had distributed more than 77,000 copies of the official Celebration poster for the store windows and bulletin boards of well-wishers throughout the city.

[3] In six weeks, New Yorkers would go to the polls, electing as mayor Tammany-supported reform Democrat William Jay Gaynor. In a three-way race, Gaynor won 43% of the vote, handily defeating millionaire newspaper publisher William Randolph Hearst (Independent, 26%).

[4] The 1909 Alaska-Yukon-Pacific Exposition was being held on the West Coast.

# CHAPTER VIII

## *NIEUWE ROTTERDAMSCHE COURANT*

New York, Sunday, September 23, 1909

Exclusive Dispatch

### THE HUDSON-FULTON CELEBRATION

WE CAN NOW REPORT on last night's formal dinner at the imposing St. Regis Hotel, hosted for the Netherlands delegation by New York's Dutch Club and the Dutch Chamber of Commerce. Among the guests were staff officers of H.M.S. *Utrecht*. Surely all present will remember with pleasure this international event. Toasts were offered in English, in deference to the many American guests in the ballroom, but emphasizing our Dutch camaraderie. This typical Dutch atmosphere was made apparent when the toastmaster, Baron Jonkheer Loudon, Dutch Ambassador to the United States, introduced the president of New York's Hudson-Fulton Commission, the U.S. Civil War veteran, General Stewart L. Woodford. The diners responded with a rendition of "Lang zal ze leven in de gloria." Only this reporter's presence at the press table prevented this morning's newspapers from printing that the group had sung the Dutch national anthem at General Woodford. But *The New York Times* reporter understood the meaning of the "Lang zal hij leven" when he headlined his article by noting that those present serenaded the aging but still robust general with a "very Dutch version of "For he's a jolly good fellow." General Woodford seemed taken with the song, after his table mate, Amsterdam mayor van Leeuwen, explained to him what it was all about.

The tasteful decorations included the princely colors, the national tricolor, and a large oil portrait of Her Majesty, the Queen, which had been presented earlier to the Dutch Club of New York. Flowers in wicker baskets shaped like half moons adorned each table as centerpieces, while every guest found two small "wooden" shoes created in porcelain next to his plate, as a souvenir from the hotel.

The cover of the handsomely designed menu showed the *Halve-Maen* flanked by the Dutch and American flags, while the back cover bore a picture of Lower Manhattan. The audience seemed pleased when General Woodford, in a humorous remark, pointed to this picture of New York with its skyscrapers and exclaimed, "Every time I return to Holland I marvel at how flat our countryside is, but here you have the 'flat-land of Nieuw Amsterdam.' " His play on words noted how most New Yorkers live in so-called "flats."

To complete our description of the hotel ballroom decorations, we should also mention that both sides of the ballroom were covered with windmills, which even from far away bore little resemblance to the ones in Holland. The music consisted almost entirely of old Dutch songs which of course pleased all of us Dutchmen.

A few comments about the speeches of the evening:
Ambassador Loudon briefly recounted the history of the Netherlands' long fight for independence from Spain; the Dutch mastery of the seas and especially the arrival of Henry Hudson in America. He bemoaned the stubborn and often useless fighting that Holland had to endure more than once to maintain its independence. "It is often necessary to fight for independence," he said, "and when we achieve it, we must fight to keep it." At the end of his speech, Baron Loudon praised the efforts of General Woodford, J. T. Cremer, and many others. Following a good Dutch custom, the ambassador raised his glass in a toast to those two hardworking gentlemen.

Mr. Cremer then explained the economic importance of the Netherlands to the rest of the world. He said that he and his friends were very pleased to have received such a hospitable welcome from the community of Dutch merchants, so far from home. "We are here in the sense of a trade delegation," Mr. Cremer continued, "which is why I want to talk to you about trade tonight." He did this in a very amusing way, hailing the Dutch commerce of the past; how they once were the freight carriers of Europe; how they battled Spain and Portugal in Indonesia and the Americas—and won; and how all this resulted in trade expansion and the creation of settlements in the most important places in the world. A period of national decline then set in, during which Holland regrettably lost many of its international possessions. "Frankly," said the Ambassador, "we grew too rich."

Meanwhile, foreigners who had always sought traditional Dutch hospitality and freedom from the religious persecution of other lands became as successful as their Dutch hosts in the development of their own businesses.

Mr. Cremer pointed with gratitude to the historic significance of Holland. "We don't live off old glory; we try to acquire fresh new glory." This sentiment won the applause of all present. Mr. Cremer also pointed out how Holland had to recruit its army from among merchant men, sea captains, and the navy. He then spoke of the significance of the Dutch trade at this time. It is probably unnecessary to mention that Mr. Cremer's speech, which ended with a commendation about both the trade and entrepreneurship of the Dutch, was well received by the audience.

Additional speakers were Mayor van Leeuwen—introduced by Baron Loudon as the "Pieter Stuyvesant" of today's Amsterdam—Messrs. Stuyvesant Fish, John Kean, S. P. van Eeghen, Colonel van Hecking-Colenbrander, and J. R. Planten, who all expressed well wishes both for Her Majesty the Queen and Princess Juliana. Mr. A. Gijn, local agent for the Holland-America Line and member of the Halve-Maen Committee, received a hearty ovation when the Ambassador announced that Her Majesty had appointed Mr. Gijn to `Ridder in de Orde van Oranje-Nassau.'

It did not escape unnoticed to some Americans that reference was being made only to the "Hudson" portion of the festivities.

General Woodford spoke next, praised Holland, and detailed what the Dutch, especially in their earliest years had meant to America and how the first leaders of the English settlement in Massachusetts had received their formal education at the University of Leiden. His humorous speech showed a great familiarity with our history and ended with a toast to Her Majesty, the Queen.

All those present joined in sending the following cablegram:

"To Her Majesty, the Queen, Den Haag— The Netherlands. At the suggestion of General Stewart L. Woodford, president of the Hudson-Fulton commission, Dutchmen and Americans from New York, the Dutch Halve Maen Committee, the Commander and crew of the cruiser *Utrecht,* all assembled at a dinner party given by the Dutch Chamber of Commerce and the Dutch Club of New York at the St. Regis, respectfully present you our greetings on the opening of the Hudson-Fulton festivities."

This morning this reply was received—

"By order of Her Majesty, I transfer sincere thanks to General Stewart L. Woodford and all who sent greetings which Her Majesty highly appreciates.
—W. G. Schimmelpenninck."

---

EXTRACT FROM THE OFFICIAL NEW YORK STATE HISTORY (1910)
OF THE HUDSON-FULTON CELEBRATION:

OPENING on the 1 September and lasting through the middle of December, the New York Botanical Garden in the Bronx mounted a special indoor-outdoor exhibition, covering more than 200 acres, and open daily during the Hudson-Fulton Celebration. The Garden's magnificent collection of trees, plants, shrubs, and natural woodland was highlighted by a decorative cardboard "H" denoting those specimens that were growing anywhere in the Hudson River Valley at the time of the explorer's visit in 1609.

# CHAPTER IX

## *NIEUWE ROTTERDAMSCHE COURANT*

New York, Sunday, September 24, 1909

Exclusive Dispatch

### THE HUDSON-FULTON CELEBRATION

AS SOON AS the formal transfer of the *Halve-Maen* to the people of the City of New York had taken place, signaling the start of the Celebration, Lieutenant William Lam ran up the Dutch flag on the replica. His action set off a salvo of cannon fire from the warships in the river, accompanied by rousing cheers from the crowds along the waterfront and the singing of *"Wilhelmus van Nassau-wen."*

The Holland-America Line's passenger flagship *Nieuw Amsterdam* had arrived in New York with its contingent of Dutch participants. These guests joined in the transfer festivities, followed by a reception aboard the cruiser *Utrecht*.

In the evening, the Holland Society hosted a $20-a-plate banquet in the Grand Ballroom of the Waldorf-Astoria Hotel to honor the entire Dutch delegation. For clarification, the Holland Society is a totally different organization from the Hollandische Club, which is a group of Dutchmen living in New York City. The Society is a corporate body of distinguished Americans who can trace their lineage to Holland or a Dutch ancestor.

The large ballroom of the Waldorf-Astoria, accommodating 260 guests, was handsomely decorated with the Stars and Stripes next to the Dutch tricolor. Above the dais with the guests of honor, hung the orange flag of the Holland Society. It was a grand night, and the speeches were received with great applause, especially the one given by Mayor van Leeuwen of Amsterdam. Mr. P. van

Druzer, president of the Holland Society and toastmaster for the evening, offered an after-dinner toast to the Queen, President Taft, and the Dutch people in general.

In addition to Messrs. van Leeuwen and Druzer, the following gentlemen also said a few words: Mr. S. P. van Eeghen, president of the Dutch Hudson-Fulton committee; Mr. J. T. Cremer, representative of the Dutch government; Mr. Boissevain, president of the Dutch Chamber of Commerce in the United States; retired American judge Augustus van Wyck; and Mr. Warner van Norden. Seated at the table of honor were, the Reverend Dr. Kittredge, president of the St. Nicholas Society; Mr. E. P. de Monchy, president of the Rotterdam Chamber of Commerce; Colonel van Hecking-Colenbrander of the *Utrecht*; J. R. Planten; Captain J. B. Mardook of the U.S. Navy; C. Heldring, the banker; Herbert S. Satterles; R. van Does; and Consul-General P. R. Plaaten.

Mr. Cremer responded to the diner's toast to the Queen by reporting on Her Majesty's status as a new mother. He indicated her great interest in the Celebration. He also mentioned the amount of respect President Taft enjoys in our country, even though, according to Mr. Cremer, he has only recently succeeded President Roosevelt, we know that he is a person of great integrity and competence. We also know that he will be successful in enriching the people of this land, as well as others, and that he will strive to maintain both peace and understanding between all nations.

A congratulatory message has also been sent by the Society to Her Majesty, who responded through the government with the following cablegram: "THE QUEEN DESIRES ME TO CONVEY HER MAJESTY'S SINCERE THANKS TO THE HOLLAND SOCIETY OF NEW YORK FOR THEIR LOYAL MESSAGE FOR HER HOUSE AND NATION." (signed: van Geon)

Mr. van Wyck impressed upon his Dutch guests that there was a deep feeling of friendship, affection, and firm pride that the members of the Holland Society felt for what the Dutch accomplished during their glorious history, to the present. He voiced the hope that world peace would never be disturbed, but if it unexpectedly ever was, there would be feelings of assistance between the Dutch and the Americans, as was the case in Holland during the American Revolution in 1776.

Great laughter erupted when Mr. van Wyck mentioned that Holland was so small that for every new baby born, some other Dutchman had to leave the country (laughter), and that for this reason the Dutch, whether they are seafarers, merchants, or bankers, can be found in all parts of the world. The general air of bonhomie at this international gathering, he said, effectively buried the old canard of that English schoolboy taunt:

> *In matters commercial*
> *The fault of the Dutch*
> *Was giving so little*
> *While asking so much*!

(Laughter) Mr. van Wyck ended his loudly applauded speech with the words: "May the Queen live long and happily, and rule wisely."

————————————————————

### EXTRACT FROM THE OFFICIAL NEW YORK STATE HISTORY (1910) OF THE HUDSON-FULTON CELEBRATION:

FROM THE WHITE HOUSE, two months after the end of the Celebration, President Taft finally sent a letter to the Commission which said, in part: "In response to your letter, I beg to thank you for the official gold medal struck by your Commission. I congratulate you upon the great success of this celebration which you inaugurated and carried out." The President surrendered the medal to the State Department.

# CHAPTER X

## *NIEUWE ROTTERDAMSCHE COURANT*

New York, Sunday, September 25, 1909

Exclusive Dispatch

### THE HUDSON-FULTON CELEBRATION

TO THEIR PLEASANT SURPRISE, the millions of people in and around New York who planned to attend the Hudson-Fulton Celebration rose up this morning to a beautiful clear day and an azure sky. They could not have wished for more pleasant weather to open the Celebration.

Beyond any doubt, the lower end of the Hudson River creates a spectacular stage for what has been planned. Grandstands have been constructed on both sides of this "American Rhine," with an expansive view of the river. On the eastern shore of the Hudson between 72nd Street in Manhattan and Spuyten Duyvil Creek in the Bronx, lies Riverside Park with beautiful trees and green grassy hillsides. And right across on the west bank of the river, in the State of New Jersey, between Hoboken and Englewood Cliffs, are the towering rocky walls of the Palisades.

Early this morning, thousands of people gathered and descended to both banks of the river, especially near the Hudson-Fulton Gate of Honor, close to the official reviewing stand.

Today, this wonderful river, bearing the name of its world-renowned discoverer, looked most agreeable. Its broad surface displayed a pleasant blue tint, while the rains of the past few days made the greenery along the banks look even brighter.

GOVERNMENTS from all over the world have sent ambassadors and other dignitaries to this memorable event. Their ships of war and other vessels are now anchored in an impressive chainlike array measuring 10 English miles, or 16,100 meters. From all the visits exchanged in the morning between the naval officers of the various nations, it was quite apparent that those huge "sea castles" were here for an unwarlike occasion.

All vessels on the mighty blue Hudson, no matter what their nature, were flying the official flag—the oranje-blanje-bleu tricolor that speaks of Holland's most famous seagoing era. The reviewing stand near the Hudson-Fulton Gate was dressed in orange, a color so dear to us. It is the color that has been a theme in all the decorations, whether worn by partygoers, flown on flags, or in the programs of festivities. It is clear that great homage has been paid to Holland. Right across from the Hudson River reviewing stand is the armored cruiser *H.M.S. Utrecht*, anchored next to the Holland-America Steamship Company's new *Amsterdam*. The *Utrecht*, dressed in white, contrasts with the blue water and looks impressive compared to the new *Amsterdam*, and the American naval training ship *Portsmouth*. The Dutch naval officers, led by Colonel van Hecking-Colenbrander, are keeping the name of the Old Fatherland in high view, as are the "Jantjes."[1]

At the invitation of Colonel van Leent we were privileged, especially on a day like this, to set foot again on "Dutch soil" and to enjoy the hospitality aboard the *Utrecht*. Starting at nine in the morning, motor sloops carried the public to the *Utrecht*, back and forth all day. It was almost midnight before the last guests, mesmerized by the nighttime beauty of the river, were ferried ashore in launches from the *Nieuw Amsterdam*.

**Plate 10:** *Half-Moon* **towed by tug to Naval Parade.**

THE BIG MOMENT came at 3:30 in the afternoon when the *Halve-Maen* sailed up the Hudson from Staten Island. She was accompanied by Uncle Sam's torpedo boats and smaller craft as well as the sound of saluting guns and the singing of "Vien Neerlands Bloed" and the "Wilhelmus van Nassau-wen." Bowing to headwinds, Lieutenant William Lam, commander of the *Halve-Maen*, decided not to put his craft under sail. Instead, pulled by a tugboat, it passed the reviewing stand amid deafening cheers and applause.

It was a solemn moment as the *Halve-Maen* was finally transferred to the American Commission. Its president, General Woodford, expressed great appreciation for this Dutch present, which was the most welcome of all the formal gifts. Mr. S. P. van Eeghen also spoke very eloquently during the transfer, pointing out how proud Holland was that its sons had been the founders of what used to be called "Nieuw Nederland." The Dutch, he said, were also the people who provided shelter for the Puritans until they left Delft for Massachusetts, to colonize New England. Old Holland thus played a big role in the establishment of the New England provinces.

Lieutenant Lam and his crew, dressed in ancient Dutch attire, as was Mr. Benthem, the Dutch builder of the replicated *Halve-Maen*, drew much attention. When the bearded officer, dressed as Hudson, appeared on board the *Utrecht* along with his wife, who had crossed the sea for this special occasion, a vociferous cheer broke out and ll guns saluted.

At this point, while "Henry Hudson" clambered into a rowboat to go ashore, the *Clermont* was the subject of another tribute.

This exact replica of Fulton's steamship, which indeed for most Americans is of great historic importance, came up the river under its own steam power. One

**Plate 11: Stern View of *Clermont*.**

**Plate 12: The *Clermont* replica in Upper Bay, September 25, 1909.**

cannot help but be impressed when one realizes how important this relatively tiny and awkward splinter of a ship, the first of its kind, was to the future of river and oceanic navigation all over the world.

After Henry Hudson (Lieutenant Lam) came ashore and introduced himself to the waiting Dutch gentlemen, they all walked from the floating pier across a connecting gangplank to the reviewing stand, followed by those aboard the *Clermont*. The head of the American Celebration Commission, General Woodford, stood with U.S. Vice-President James S. Sherman (who was present during most of the activities), New York Governor Charles Evans Hughes, and many others.[2] They listened to a speech by Mr. S. P. van Eeghen, whose voice carried a good distance and which from time to time met with audible approval.

He said, in part:

The Dutch Hudson-Fulton Celebration Commission have bestowed on me the honor to represent them here today and it is therefore with great pleasure that I address all of you. Our festivities commemorate that bold seafarer Henry Hudson, who 300 years ago, as an employee of the Dutch East India Company, laid the foundation for what is now the most important city in the United States. This celebration has also created a lively interest all over Holland.

The Dutch people are very proud of those farsighted "burghers" from the Republic of the United Netherlands who were so influential in the creation of this New York metropolis once known as "New Amsterdam." One must also remember that many of those who offered their lives and property in the fight for freedom and independence for the new United States of America were of solid Dutch ancestry. In addition, many of Holland's sons and daughters who crossed the ocean, and whose descendants are dwelling here peacefully, form a lively link between Holland and the United States of America regarding religious and political freedom, commerce and industry, and science and art.

In an effort to appropriately express our feelings in tangible form to the greatest and most powerful nation in the world, the Dutch, under the patronage of His Majesty Prinz Hendrik of the Netherlands, took up our role with the Hudson-Fulton Celebration Commission whose goal was to present its sister committee in New York with a copy as close as possible to the original *Halve-Maen*, the ship that sailed three centuries ago from Amsterdam, crossing the ocean to the river that now bears its Captain's name.

May the American Hudson-Fulton Celebration Commission now accept our replica of this little ship, this nutshell, whose arrival in these waters eventually played such an important part in the development of the United States. As proof of the closeness that we continue to feel for each other, I now have the honor on behalf of the Dutch members of the Hudson-Fulton Celebration Commission to present you with the *Halve-Maen*, along with a document confirming the gift and ask that you accept her and this book, which contains the names of all those who contributed to this enterprise.

The Linschoten organization, whose members collect old ship journals of our courageous seafarers and publish them in book form, has now requested me to present their first volume to the Hudson-Fulton Celebration Commission. This book contains the journal of Jan Cornelius May, who in 1611 made the same journey as Hudson did two years earlier. I have the honor to present this book to you on their behalf and ask you to please accept it.

General Woodford answered:

The Hudson-Fulton Celebration Commission appreciates everything that our friends and relatives from Holland have done to celebrate this 300th birthday of our City. We greet you with tender friendship. We hope that you will enjoy this magnificent City, grown from an acorn planted by our forefathers, to a majestic oak, we welcome you now into our hearts and our homes. All of New York wishes Holland the greatest prosperity, and may the richest blessings of Heaven forever rest upon the brow of your fair young Queen.

Turning toward "Henry Hudson," and addressing him with a humorous, "Monsieur le Capitaine," General Woodford continued with deliberation:

The questions of precedence plays an important role as fleets from various nations meet each other. But here today, Captain Hudson has risen from his grave to welcome all of us.

With this, the Hudson portion of the opening day's official Hudson-Fulton ceremony came to a close.

Still waiting aboard the *Clermont* were the famous engineer with his bride "Mary Livingston," and other members of their group, dressed in beautiful period costumes of 100 years ago. They all stepped ashore, to be greeted by General Woodford. The General mentioned that it was almost 300 years since he had spoken to "Henry Hudson," but that he still felt young enough to say a few words of welcome to "Robert Fulton." To which "Mr. Fulton" bowed and gravely replied, "Although the prospect of personal emolument has been some inducement to me, yet I feel infinitely more pleasure in reflecting on the numerous advantages that my country will derive from my invention."

Following this, the special delegate from Japan, Prince Kuniyoshi Kuni, read a beautifully designed proclamation in which the Japanese people living in New York thanked the Commission for their decision to accept their gift of 2,100 cherry trees to be planted along Riverside Drive. General Woodford answered with friendly words, to the delight of all assembled. With a "thank you" to all present, the Hudson-Fulton festivities were officially open.

The day ended with a stunning display of fireworks. The Dutch are often flabbergasted by stories about America. It is possible that only a person as articulate as our well-known Dutch novelist Israel Querido would be able to describe the true mystery of the wide river and the festive impression made by illuminated ships, the buildings all strung together on lines of light, the searchlights on the towers in the City, and the glowing warships. A visiting merchant from Rotterdam told us that he only could think of two words to describe the experience, "brilliant" and "marvelous." That probably was an understatement.

---

### EXTRACT FROM THE OFFICIAL NEW YORK STATE HISTORY (1910) OF THE HUDSON-FULTON CELEBRATION:

AT 10:30 AM, several divisions of the Grand Naval Parade had assembled with the *Half-Moon* and *Clermont* in Staten Island's Kill van Kull Channel. During the rest of the morning and early afternoon, they maneuvered along the northern shore of Staten Island and the Bay Ridge shore of Long Island, in order to give the citizens of Richmond and Brooklyn boroughs at least a sighting of these two tiny but famous vessels.

Soon after the *Half-Moon* and *Clermont* left their anchorages to join this parade, the former moving under her own sails and the latter propelled by her own steam power, the engine of the *Clermont* suddenly slipped a cam setscrew on the valve-gear rocker shaft, and she came to a stop to make the necessary repairs.

While the Clermont" lay-to, the *Half-Moon*, frisky as a racehorse in the starting gate, bore down on the *Clermont's* starboard quarter. Unable to avoid the steam-

Plate 13:  The two centerpieces collide. The *Half-Moon* rams the *Clermont*,
September 25, 1909.
Plate 14: Saluting the Naval Parade, Riverside Park.

**Plate 15: Official Naval Parade Landing at Riverside Park and 110th Street.**

boat, the *Half-Moon* rammed her just abaft the boiler, breaking her rail, tearing away a stanchion, and staving in a plank below the wearing piece. The *Half-Moon*'s figurehead and some of her stays were carried away. For a time the *Half-Moon* was locked in the *Clermont's* unexpected embrace, in a jumble of sails and anchors.

Meanwhile the harbor tug, *Dalzelline*, assisting in clearing the decks of the *Half-Moon*, collided with her main boom, snapping it off at the sheet. The collision of the two replicas caused more amusement than damage. Repairs were quickly made, and the flotilla soon proceeded on its way up the Hudson towards Grant's Tomb[3] followed by the warship contingent led by Pierpont Morgan's yacht *Corsaire*. From the very start, the replicas were the objects of continuous cannon salutes, some from shore guns that had not been fired for a century, to which the *Half-Moon* responded by firing back with her own little falcon [cannon].

# NOTES

[1]Nickname for Dutch sailors.

[2]Former Columbia Law professor Hughes operated in the halls of power through most of his life. Following his governorship, he was defeated for president by Woodrow Wilson, served as Secretary of State under Warren Harding, and was appointed Chief Justice of the U.S. Supreme Court by Herbert Hoover.

[3] Sited at Riverside Drive and 122nd Street, it is the final resting place of the brilliant Civil War General and his wife, Julia Dent Grant. The structure, designed by architect John Duncan and completed in 1897, is a curious and eclectic melange of Greco-Roman architectural motifs, executed in good old New England granite. Grant is the only President buried in New York City, and his tomb is the second largest mausoleum in the Western Hemisphere.

# CHAPTER XI

## *NIEUWE ROTTERDAMSCHE COURANT*

New York, Sunday, September 26, 1909

Exclusive Dispatch

### THE HUDSON-FULTON CELEBRATION

LAST NIGHT, the Hudson River looked more beautiful than ever, as the warships, Riverside Park, and the Jersey side of the river were all illuminated. Today's warships may not have the same elegance as the sailing ships of yesteryear, but the sight produced by these dozen or so warships, illuminated from top to bottom, was spellbinding. Even though the rest of the city had also bathed itself in lights, Riverside Park became the focal point of the event, especially near the Hudson-Fulton triumphal arch at the water gate below Grant's Tomb.

It seemed as if tens of thousands of spectators who may have missed many of the festivities during the day had all come out to celebrate as night fell. Three hours after we left the park, we returned, only to discover that the number of spectators and motor cars on the streets had increased tenfold. Thanks to precautionary arrangements, there were no disturbances of any kind in the city. There were even fewer accidents yesterday than on any normal day.

At about 8:30 pm, the first fireworks exploded over the Jersey side of the river. It was a beautiful display of colors that even the Americans, who are spoiled when it comes to fireworks, could admire. It was a fascinating, fairylike evening, full of charm. To be honest, earlier in the day some beautiful fireworks had already been discharged as the *Halve-Maen* and the *Clermont* passed the reviewing stand. Skyrockets of a brand new design, created enormous umbrella-like

**Plate 16: Illumination of Official Landing.**
**Plate 17: Illumination of warships.**

**Plate 18: Celebration fireworks at Grant's Tomb.**

showers of feathery white light against New York's beautiful deep blue sky, so different from all other smoke-spewing industrial cities.

From the reviewing stand one could see the 57 illuminated naval vessels of various nations. One was reminded of the similar festive decorations at the lakes of the Haagsche Bosch.[1]

After a swift evening trip by steam sloop to H.M.S. *Utrecht*, with a hospitable welcome by its captain and officers, it became easy to see the outline of all the other warships. At the center of our ship we saw the name *Utrecht* spelled out in electrically illuminated letters several feet high. Close by lay the British H.M.S. *Inflexible*, whose gray coat made it hardly distinguishable during the day. It now was attracting all eyes, thanks to a twinkling electrical depiction of the British crown in a jeweled setting. While all the warships competed with each other, it was the totality of the spectacle that was so impressive.

This "festival of lights" was made even more lustrous thanks to the beautiful effect of many powerful searchlights. Twenty such lights had been set up around 153rd Street, with the total strength of fifty million candles. Four light beams continually crisscrossed each other to beautifully illuminate the proud dome of

**Plate 19: Illumination of
Washington Square Arch.**

General Grant's Tomb. But this was
not the only place where light displays fascinated the eye; all the
bridges crossing the East River
were handsomely outlined. Even
the new Manhattan Bridge, not yet
open to traffic, connecting Brooklyn with Manhattan, situated
slightly north of the Brooklyn
Bridge, sparkled in a way that
clearly displayed its striking shape.

Although the Brooklyn Bridge
wears the largest number of light
bulbs (13,000) in its hair, it is the
new Queensboro Bridge from 59th
Street to Long Island City, with its
all-steel, less than solid-looking
construction, that far surpasses her
sister bridges with its pleasing
lines. Garlands of lights accentuated this appearance.

Dating back to Robert Fulton's
day and now surrounded by 20-
story skyscrapers and lavishly dec-
orated hotels, stands New York's brilliantly lit two-story City Hall. Sparkling
above all others was the huge tower of the Metropolitan Life Insurance Company
building, completed last year. This 30-story white marble colossus looked like a
clear shiny mass, magically appearing and disappearing in the clouds.

A mile away, competing with this sight, was the beautiful tower of the Singer
Building.[2] The fine colors of this giant structure were accentuated by the surrounding lights. Among other beautiful sights, the foot of the flatiron-shaped
Fuller Building at 23rd Street and Fifth Avenue presented a Dutch landscape, decorated in a way Americans like to think of as Dutch, with a most graceful windmill as a centerpiece.

To the north lay the "Great White Way," the section of Broadway around
which one finds the most important theaters and restaurants, and which during
normal days is already bathed in a sea of light. The Hotel Astor, the Imperial
Hotel, the New York Times Building, and the Knickerbocker Hotel—each with its
own decoration—looked marvelous.

The southeast corner of Central Park, with its clusters of trees, rock forma-
tions, and ponds offers a striking natural contrast to the artificially lit hotels outside the park wall. The Plaza Hotel, the beautiful ivory building which currently
houses the Dutch Hudson Fulton Celebration Committee stands out both by day

and night. One city monument that lends itself perfectly to being decorated with lights is the Washington Memorial Arch spanning Fifth Avenue at Washington Square Park. Countless thousands have come to view it.

As we have noted above, it was a wonderful day. And at night, no one heard any complaint from Mr. Edison's company, which sells New York City all of its electrical power.

---

## EXTRACT FROM THE OFFICIAL NEW YORK STATE HISTORY (1910) OF THE HUDSON-FULTON CELEBRATION:

PIERPONT MORGAN'S curator/companion, Belle da Costa, is quoted as saying privately,"Even though I find the whole performance disgusting I was perforce amused and a tiny wee bit excited by the electrical displays. Every building in New York and the entire Fifth Avenue is draped in a hideous combination of orange and blue and red, white and blue and at night is a fairyland thoroughfare of electric lights."

RELIGIOUS SERVICES were scheduled for all faiths accustomed to worshiping on the first day of the week.

Evening concerts included music at the Great Hall of the College of the City of New York, a concert by Irish citizens at Carnegie Hall and a concert in the Hippodrome by the United German singers of New York.

ON THIS DAY, *The New York Times* printed in full a 27-stanza poem by Joseph Ignatius Constantine Clarke. The first stanza declaims:

> *Here at thy broad sea gate,*
> *On the ultimate ocean wave,*
> *Where millions in hope have entered in,*
> *Joyous, elate,*
> *A home and a hearth to win;*
> *For the promise you held and the bounty you gave,*
> *Thou, and none other,*
> *I call to thee, spirit, I call to thee, Mother,*
> *America.*

# NOTES

[1]A famous park in The Hague.

[2]Completed in 1908, this early skyscraper towered 47 stories above Lower Broadway.

# CHAPTER XII

## *NIEUWE ROTTERDAMSCHE COURANT*

New York, Monday, September 27, 1909

Exclusive Dispatch

### THE HUDSON-FULTON CELEBRATION

YESTERDAY, many of the Dutch members of the Celebration Commission, led by Colonel van Hecking-Colenbrander and his officers, attended Sunday services at the Dutch Reformed Saint Nicholas Church on Fifth Avenue. The church was established in 1623 as one of the first structures set up by the original Dutch settlers on the island of Manhattan. The Saint Nicholas Church, like many other houses of worship, was fully decorated for the occasion with flowers and the flags of many nations. For an austere Dutchman, this required some getting used to.

SUNDAY'S EVENTS were climaxed by a grand dinner party. In addition to the Dutch contingent, other dignitaries present included United States Vice-President James S. Sherman and Mrs. Sherman, New York's Governor Charles Evans Hughes and Mrs. Hughes and their three children, as well as many other members of New York City's private and public elite. One speaker, Dr. William E. Griffis, spoke of the character of William the Silent, pointing to the positive influence he had on Hudson's voyage.

THIS AFTERNOON, a special six-car New York Central Railroad train carried the Celebration speakers and almost 500 guests from the temporary train sheds at Grand Central Station (the magnificent new terminal is still in construction) to the little Spuyten Duyvil local rail stop.

Arriving in the middle of a fall thunderstorm, we were all carried by bus and motorcar up the hill to the place where, according to the books, Hudson first met the Weckquaesgeek Indians. The purpose of our afternoon visit was to lay the cornerstone for the 100-foot high Hudson Memorial Column. The expectation is that when New York's growth requires a new bridge across Spuyten Duyvil Creek, the Hudson monument will mark its north entrance.[1]

Governor Hughes delivered one of his charming down-to-earth speeches. In the downpour, the Governor, with rain streaking his whiskers, spoke of the monument as evidence of our respect for a man who combined courage, audacity, trust, and a set of values essential to maintain the American way of life. Hudson, the Governor remarked, is one of the earliest of our heroes and an inspiration to all American men and women.

AT 8:30 THIS EVENING, the official reception took place at the Metropolitan Opera House. A long poem honoring Robert Fulton was read while everyone stood, after which the representatives of various participating nations were introduced, following an alphabetic sequence of countries. Mayor McClellan repeated, "I have the honor to introduce Mr. (name of Guest), the representative from (name of Country)." The audience vociferously applauded each introduction, and the personage in question, who had nothing to say, stood up and said, "Thank you." Those who wanted to say a few words came forward and were greeted graciously. Some representatives from the South American republics spoke in Spanish, but most speeches were in English—with the exception of M. Darboux, who not only spoke in his native tongue but also, according to a French tradition, made his speech quite a long one. Then Mayor McClellan said, "I now have the honor to introduce all of you to Mr. J. T. Cremer, special envoy of the Netherlands."

Mr. Cremer moved to the rostrum, and friendly applause arose which began again when Mr. Cremer started his speech with the words, "Her Majesty the Queen of The Netherlands. . ."  In a firm voice, he said the following: "Her Majesty the Queen of The Netherlands has charged me with the honor of conveying to the Hudson-Fulton Celebration Commission her expressions of support and those of her subjects with the memorial celebration of events of such great importance, the discovery of the Hudson River and the application of steam to the shipping industry. The flag of The Netherlands once flew over this beautiful river and over the settlements of New-Netherlands, now the proud mighty state and city of New York. The discovery was the work of energetic, entrepreneurial burghers of the Lowlands. They were hardened by their eighty-year-long fight for freedom from Spain in which the leaders, the princes of the House of Orange-Nassau, encouraged foreign trade as the country's main source of income. This river was once temporarily named after the great Dutch war hero Prince Maurits and had forts on her banks called *Oranje* and *Nassau*, facts which our Queen did not forget. The memories of those days are still very real on both sides of the ocean. Her Majesty knows that a great number of you, dignified burghers, love the country from which your forefathers came and still follow many of the old traditions. She knows that in the interest of peace and goodwill among the citizens of both countries, your people are offering their friendship to her people, and she knows too that the only official flag used by your Committee is the old flag of The Netherlands, which brings our two countries even closer together.

"Great was our sympathy for the country, which had to fight the most difficult war to gain its freedom, and for the mighty Republic of the New World during and after its own fight for independence and freedom. Her Majesty, the Queen of The Netherlands, remembers the fact that on November 17, 1776, the flag of the United States flying atop the sloop-of-war *Andrew Doria* was saluted by Fort Oranje on the West Indian Island of St. Eustatius. The Queen has charged me with presenting you with her greetings to the emblem of your magnificent decorations, our old flag which now is your flag."

A spontaneous cheer broke out in the Opera House, lasting for minutes, with the continuous waving of the silk standard of the Commission, signifying a thank you. The band played the old "Wilhelmus," with all present on their feet. Mayor McClellan then introduced the mayor of Amsterdam, Mr. W. P. van Leeuwen, who was heartily received. Mr. Van Leeuwen spoke as follows: "Mr. Mayor and dear colleagues. I did not hesitate for a moment to cross the ocean in order to bring greetings from Old Amsterdam to New Amsterdam. If I prefer to use the name which this mighty metropolis carried in its youth, it is not only because this name calls into memory historical facts that delight every Dutchman, but more so because the name signifies a three-century-old friendship between our two countries (Applause). I know very well that the Amsterdam Office of the East-India Company did not send out the *Halve-Maen* to discover new territories in North America and that Hudson's discovery of the river named after him may have been pure luck. However, in those days, the entrepreneurial Dutch equipped their ships to take advantage of any discoveries like Hudson's and started trading with newly created settlements, resulting in situations like New Amsterdam and New-Netherlands.

"Among these trading ships was the *Tijger* [Tiger] from Amsterdam under command of the well known Captain Adriaen Block. Unfortunately, his ship caught fire in the fall of 1613, just as it was being readied for its return voyage to Holland.[2]

This was indeed a great disappointment for the Dutch, who did not come here just for their health (thunderous laughter). If Block and his men had been reflective, a quality which your Washington Irving bestowed on the Dutch in general, then they might have reflected on their misfortune for the entire winter, with their hands in their pockets and their pipes in their mouths (laughter). In reality, they immediately went to work building a new ship sufficiently large enough to re-cross the ocean and by the spring of the following year it was ready and launched.

"It was prophetic that the first product to be built, or rebuilt, on this island was a ship. Because it is ships that, in the three centuries behind us, formed the bridge between this and other countries, and this will continue to be so for centuries to come, unless the airplane takes its place (much Laughter). It was also prophetic when the Dutch boat builders named the little replacement vessel *Onrust*. They were most likely trying to express the circumstances under which the ship was built. But *Onrust* not only means `unrest' but also `restless.' Restlessness, as endless energy, is a property that seems most appropriate for New York. The endless energy with which most of the citizens of this city have since been identified, has enabled it to become the metropolis that it is and which has created great admiration from visitors. In every aspect, this metropolis has become part of the most powerful and wealthiest country in the world (Applause).

"Holland and especially Amsterdam, old and new, is very pleased with this development. Old Amsterdam is proud to have laid the first small foundation for this city. I therefore would like to be the first to present to you Old Amsterdam's best and heartfelt good wishes (Applause). May the word `restless,' which until now has been the motto of this city, continue in perpetuity. May this city continue to flourish both to the advantage of the United States of America and for the well-being of humanity in general."

Messrs. McClellan, Woodford, and many of the diplomats shook Mayor Van Leeuwen's hand in appreciation for his wonderful speech. The orchestra played "Wien Nederlandsch Bloed,"[3] with everyone standing.

---

EXTRACT FROM THE OFFICIAL NEW YORK STATE HISTORY (1910)
OF THE HUDSON-FULTON CELEBRATION:

AT 11:00 AM., at Alpine, New Jersey, the long-planned Palisades Interstate Park was formally dedicated under the auspices of the Palisades Interstate Park Commission. The Commission consisted of ten members, five from New York and five from New Jersey. One immediate result of this 33-mile long "strip park" running north on the west bank of the Hudson was a definite improvement in river views and scenery. The dedication was followed by a luncheon reception at Governor's Island at the Headquarters of the Eastern Department of the United States Army.

MUSICAL EVENTS during the day and evening included: the New York Banks' Glee Club, the United German Singers at the 13th Regiment armory in Brooklyn Borough, the United German Singers of Long Island at Schutzenpark in Queens Borough; the United German Singers of Staten Island in Richmond Borough, at the Happyland Park, South Beach; and the German Singing Society's Chorus of schoolchildren, in Crotona Park in Bronx Borough.

On Staten Island, there was a historical parade at Stoneybrook, with cere-

monies at the first church built on Staten Island founded by the Waldencians commemorating the first permanent settlement on the island.

IN PREPARATION for the Fulton side of the Celebration, 90-year-old Julia Ward
Howe[4] read a six stanza poem written for the Celebration.

FULTON

*A River, flashing like a gem,*
*Crowned with a mountain diadem,*
*Invites an unaccustomed guest*
*To launch his shallop on her crest;*
*A pilgrim whose exploring mind*
*Must leave his tardy behind.*
*"My bark creep slow, the world is vast.*
*How shall its space be overpassed?"*

(plus five additional stanzas)

# NOTES

[1]Today's Henry Hudson Parkway is carried over Spuyten Duyvil Creek on a two-deck
fixed-anchor bridge, begun 26 years later and opened to the public in 1936, at a cost of $5
million. In 1909, the estimated cost for the monument presented few problems: DFl
250,000 were raised for the project.

[2]After rescuing their rigging, Block's terrified crew was able to beach the flaming *Tiger* in
a nearby inlet. They then became the first Dutchmen to winter over on Manhattan Island.
In 1916, 303 years later (and seven years after Mayor Van Leeuwen's speech) workmen
excavating a cut-and-cover tunnel for the new 7th Avenue subway discovered the charred
remains of the *Tiger*'s hull at the corner of Dey and Greenwich Streets, almost a half mile
inland from the present Hudson shoreline. The keel now rests in the collection of the
Museum of the City of New York. In 1967, the discovery site was subsumed in the deep
foundations for the doomed World Trade Center.

[3]"Whose Dutch Blood."

[4]Author of the classic Civil War lyric "The Battle Hymn of the Republic," set to the tune
of "John Brown's Body."

# CHAPTER XIII

# *NIEUWE ROTTERDAMSCHE COURANT*

New York, Tuesday, September 28, 1909

Exclusive Dispatch

## THE HUDSON-FULTON CELEBRATION

ACROSS FROM THE NEW YORK PUBLIC LIBRARY is an enormous Grecian-style porti-co, the Committee's official grandstand, the "Court of Honor" on Fifth Avenue. In this reviewing area from 40th to 42nd Street on both sides of the avenue are Corinthian columns, crowned with gilded globes and connected by green gar-lands lit at night. The space between the columns is tastefully decorated with real greens and flowers.

It was here that the elite involved in the festivities gathered to view the his-torical pageant. Among them were Messrs. Hughes, Sherman, Woodford, Le Pord, Van Koester, Seymour, and many others. Directly behind them one could hear chimes from a miniature bell tower erected for the occasion. In addition to singing "America," which is considered more suitable than the "Star Spangled Banner," one could also hear the "Wacht am Rhein," "Wien Nederlandsche Bloed," the "Marseillaise," the "Wilhelmus van Nassauen" and other national anthems.

At about three o'clock in the afternoon, the leading contingent of the parade came into view. To give an idea of the parade's length, it was close to five o'clock when the last marchers passed in review. New Yorkers called this the most beau-tiful and grand parade New York had ever seen, overshadowing the famous Columbus Day parades. Taking into account that any new "event" is often called the greatest and most beautiful, one must nevertheless agree this parade made an everlasting impression. The Dutch spectators were probably the most impressed,

**Plate 20: Fifth Avenue Court of Honor by night.**
**Plate 21: Historical Parade assembling at Central Park West and 110th Street.**

**Plate 22: Historical Parade passing the Court of Honor.**

as so many of the parade's passing floats made them think of their country and its history. Only in democratic countries where there are less conventional ideas and prejudices is it possible for both rich and poor to be part of the same parade. It is therefore a special experience for a Dutchman to see large groups of gentlemen clad in formal coats and top hats either marching afoot or on horseback in the same parade as working people.

Mayor McClellan and Herman Ridder walked at the head of the procession. The Mayor was greeted warmly and replied by waving his top hat and giving a friendly smile. Following them were various organizations representing foreign residents living in New York City—Irish, Poles, Hungarians, Bohemians, Italians, Scots, etc. These groups with their colorful banners and their especially beautiful costumes—the Italians with their blood-red frocks, both the Poles and Hungarians in their beautiful national costumes with Astrakhan hats and dashing plumes, the Scots in their highland kilts, playing their bagpipes, the Turks in their eastern colors—made more than a colorful spectacle, it was an expression of thankfulness to America, which had enabled them to succeed and reach a decent standard of living after having been driven, for one reason or another, to leave their homelands.

Messrs. Hughes and Sherman reviewed the entire procession standing, taking their hats off every time the banner of a new group passed by, while diplomats rose from their seats as did many other people when one of the marching bands played *"America"* as they passed the reviewing stand.

At the head of the section depicting the "Dutch Period" of New Amsterdam was a float showing the coat of arms of the Netherlands, displayed on the forward section of a ship and carried by two lions. When the band that headed the procession played the "Wilhelmus" everyone rose.

The next float portrayed *De Halve-Maen* manned by sailors in period costumes with the flag of the City of Amsterdam flying atop the mast and the Dutch tricolor from the stern. Behind it came "The Doomed Fate Of Henry Hudson," showing a mutinous crew in 1611 pushing Hudson off his ship toward the frigid shore of Hudson's Bay.

The fourth float in the "Dutch Period" section showed Adriaen Block and his men busy rebuilding their first ship *De Onrust* on Manhattan Island, replacing the *Tijger* which was destroyed by fire, an incident unknown to most New Yorkers. (Mayor van Leeuwen had underscored the importance of this fact in his humorous speech the day before.)

The fifth float dramatized the purchase of Manhattan Island by Peter Minuit in 1626. There under an oak tree was the first Governor of New Netherland negotiating with a number of Indian chiefs. As we all know, they agreed on a price—clothes made from flax and some other trinkets worth $24.

The next float dealt with the peace treaty with the Indians, signed in 1642 by Jonas Bronck. It depicted Bronck seated at an unfinished table with friends in the parlor of his house. In his yard, next to an old-fashioned wooden water pump, were a number of pigs searching for food. The display looked so real that one could almost mistake the sound of the wagon wheels and springs for the grunts of the animals. The name of Jonas Bronck, who in 1639 purchased land from the Indians, is eternalized in a section of New York City now called "The Bronx."

The float depicting "Peter Stuyvesant Receiving Guests" was picturesque. The fourth and most famous of the Governors-General stood on the steps of his estate home with his wooden leg, which replaced the one he had lost in the battle to conquer the island of St. Maarten. He welcomed his guests, dressed in a dark velvet jacket, a snow-white collar, and an orange sash.

The next float, "Bowling on the Bowling Green," was also enjoyable. This display drew more attention because of its bowling game than the typical old Dutch, Van Goyen-like little windmill, that was part of the same scene. It surprised us that the otherwise practical Americans had not linked the axles of the wagon to the sails of the windmill, which would have made the windmill turn while the wagon was in motion. One of the bowlers, therefore, had to push the wings now and then and be careful not to get hit by the sail.

The following float, "Dutch Doorway," displayed a very real-looking old farmhouse, the date 1679 showing on one of its side walls, with old-fashioned small windows, a square chimney, and a weather vane. Even the Lakenvelder cows looked real, and never did a milkmaid have such an easy job milking a cow. She had been picked for her Dutch beauty. We are all aware that Americans like pretty girls. When this float passed the reviewing stand, someone in the Alderman's section yelled, "Gee! Pipe the merry little milkmaid," after which a chorus of New Yorkers and Dutchmen familiar with the tune sang, "I love my wife, but oh, you kid." The milkmaid blushed and, without looking up, went on with her business.

One of the last floats showed how New Amsterdam became "New York" and how the Dutch government was eventually driven out of New Amsterdam by the victorious British in 1664.

Last but not least, to close this "Dutch Period," was a handsome portrayal of

**Plate 23: Historical Parade floats:**
**Above: Saint Nicholas.**
**Top: New Amsterdam becomes New York.**

the legendary St. Nicholas. Unfortunately the symbolic good Saint, and his black helper, Peter, as we know them in Holland, did not survive the trip across the ocean. In their place was the American "Santa Claus," in a sleigh drawn by reindeer, traveling through the snow of an ice-covered landscape. He showed the children along the parade route the toys he had for them, but they could only look, not touch.

The mammoth procession consisting of at least 54 floats cost an estimated 750,000 Dutch florins. Everything dealt with separate time periods in American history. Paraders who were not part of the float displays followed them on foot.

Father Knickerbocker, Washington Irving's "patron saint" of New York City, sauntered back and forth at the end of the line, thanking all the nations present for their participation.

THE DAY had started with an important ceremony for the Dutch. A bronze plaque in memory of seven schoolteachers who taught on the island of Manhattan during Dutch rule had been placed in a wall at New York University and now was unveiled and dedicated. After Mr. Mitchell McCracken, the president and chancellor of New York University, had made a few introductory remarks, Mr. William Maxwell pulled aside the *oranje-blanje-bleu* Dutch tricolor, exposing the plaque, which reads:

"In honor of the seven public schoolteachers who taught under Dutch rule on Manhattan Island: Adam Roelandsen, Jan Cornelissen, Jan Stevensen, William Vestens, Jan de la Montagne, Harmanus van Hoboken and Evert Pietersen. MDCXXXIII-MDCLXXIV. Erected MCMIX."

At this ceremony, Baron D'Aulnis de Bourouill, professor at the University of Utrecht, said that this event had made a great impression on him and showed him that Americans were thankful for the first steps taken by the Dutch West-India Company to maintain a civilizing order in New Amsterdam. Mr. De Bourouill also pointed out how fortunate it was to have schools

**Plate 24: 1909 Memorial to early Dutch Schoolteachers, New York University.**

that provided free education to all the people. Mr. McCracken agreed, saying that the most important contribution of Dutch rule was to subsidize free public school education. "The opening of a public school," he said, "on Peter Stuyvesant's Bowery—a little east of the present University—was more or less the last official act of the old Dutch administration."

EXTRACT FROM THE OFFICIAL NEW YORK STATE HISTORY (1910)
OF THE HUDSON-FULTON CELEBRATION:

Tuesday, September 28, 1909

EACH OF THE PARADE FLOATS represented a high point in the long history of
New York City. They were not intended to be beaux arts productions, nor was it
expected that the modeling and coloring would meet any standards of fine art.
They were, however, designed and constructed by the most expert artisans available for this kind of pageant. No pains were spared to have the workmanship performed to the highest standards.

The order of the floats in the Historical Parade was somewhat disarranged by
the elements. Monday's inclement weather was such that many doubted that the
parade would actually take place. At length the U.S. Weather Bureau reassured
the Commission that the parade could take place as scheduled, but so much time
had elapsed that it was impossible to haul the floats out from their shelter and
assemble them in the chronological order of the events portrayed, without delay-
ing the parade for two or three hours more. It was decided to form the procession
as rapidly as possible, regardless of the chronological order of the floats, 54 in all.
For a while, everything was confusion. However, the correct order was listed in
the official program.

GLENN CURTISS, the aeronaut, arrived to participate in the aerial demonstrations.
His mechanics on Governor's Island had already put his new aeroplane in working condition, but no flights were scheduled until the weekend.

# CHAPTER XIV

## *NIEUWE ROTTERDAMSCHE COURANT*

New York, Wednesday, September 29, 1909

Exclusive Dispatch

### THE HUDSON-FULTON CELEBRATION

LAST NIGHT we were unable to be present at the Brooklyn Academy of Music, where both Hudson and Fulton were honored in speeches. It is our understanding that Mr. St. Clair McKelway commemorated Henry Hudson in a speech in which he pointed to the importance of the Dutch in those historic days.

"It was," he said, " the greatest contribution of the Dutch that New Netherlands, which was discovered by Hudson and founded by the Dutch, never permitted religious persecutions. Other countries have been guilty of such persecutions, but New Netherlands can be proud of never having participated. While Hudson was indeed an Englishman," Mr. McKelway said, "he was in the commercial service of the Dutch, just like the Italian discoverer John Cabot had been in the service of the English. Holland strictly limited its claims to what Hudson had discovered, and our country sent over its merchants and others who built settlements and found enough to do. The Dutch claims were recognized by all, even by England when the British summarily captured New York. The celebration of Hudson is as much Dutch as the celebration of Fulton is American."

Reverend N. McGee Waters also spoke and said many good things about the Dutch. "It is," Mr. Waters said among other things, "about time the world realizes that American history is not complete without the part played by the New York Dutch. That this often does not happen," he said, "has to do with the fact that the

Dutch worked calmly and with modesty, something the Yankee cannot claim. It was because of this that New York ceased very early to be a Dutch colony and in the 1660s became officially British. The English wrote its books and told its history."

Today, in at least 70 public schools, there are lectures with lantern slide projections pertaining to the celebration. The universities, too, are having their Hudson-Fulton day. At New York University this includes at least eight lectures. For instance, Dr. Stewart Smith pointed out that what sometimes had been called "Fulton's Folly" was soon responsible for a six-fold increase in New York City trade. Mr. S. P. van Eeghen too addressed the students and others present. He spoke of the early sailing ship connections and pointed to the economic revolution Mr. Fulton's invention had brought about. Mr. van Eeghen, mentioned that his father had owned a fleet of Dutch-built sailing ships, except for one, the *Electra*, which had been built for him in America. It took these ships about 80 days from Amsterdam to Java, around the Cape of Good Hope, while other sailing ships did it in about 100 days. Now it takes steamships only three weeks, thanks to the opening of the Suez Canal.

**Plate 25: Official Celebration banquet, Hotel Astor.**

THE WEEK'S EVENTS were highlighted by a banquet of gargantuan proportions such as New York had not often seen. That is of course only possible in a metropolis—a sit-down dinner for 2,500 people in one big ballroom at the Hotel Astor with at least 250 beautifully set tables. The Commission spared no effort to make this a perfect affair. The cost for the entire evening was more than $135,000. All the decorations in the hall were dedicated to Holland. In addition to the Dutch national colors, the walls were bedecked with Delft blue decorations. On one side of the ballroom was a depiction of landscapes and town views. On the opposite side of the hall was the Hudson River with the *Halve-Maen* and the *Clermont*, plus, for scale, a giant contemporary steamship. From the highest gallery, projecting into the hall, hung the bow of the *Halve-Maen* with reefed sails, while the bow of the *Clermont* hung from the opposite side.

The list of banquet participants, almost a book by itself, was handed to guests as they entered. The cover displayed the crest of the Celebration Commission, with the entire booklet held together by an orange, white, and blue ribbon. As we leaf through it, we find the opening pages taken up by the names of the members of the Dutch Hudson-Fulton Celebration Commission and other important officials. Following them were the names of the members of the diplomatic corps, the special representatives, as well as members of various consulates and those of the Legislature of the State of New York, and so forth.

Among the American dignitaries present were Vice President James S. Sherman; New York State Governor Charles Evans Hughes; New York City Mayor George B. McClellan; New York State Senator Elihu Root; Comptroller Herman Metz; William Loeb; Professor Campbell; John Jacob Astor; bankers J. S. Bache, August Belmont, A. G. Hodenpijl, J. Pierpont Morgan; New York Central Railroad's president Edwin Hawley; W. H. Truesdale; D. G. Reid; the president of the Steel Trust, Elbert H. Gary; and hundreds of others from important segments of science, commerce, and industry in the United States.

The mood at the banquet was delightful. The speeches during the latter part of the evening received great attention. It should be said that British Admiral Edward Seymour was greeted enthusiastically tonight as well as last Monday at the Metropolitan Opera House, which was not the case with German Admiral Hans von Koester; the not-so-subtle jockeying for national position continued. Prince Kuniyoshi Kuni too was greeted warmly by the audience and by the women, forced by convention to remain in the ballroom galleries.[1]

Messrs. Woodford, Hughes, Sherman, Seymour, and von Koester all spoke. Colonel von Hecking-Colenbrander, commander of the "Utrecht" greeted by long applause, noted the importance of Holland because the Rhine ends there. He also spoke of our coastline with its beautiful harbors, which could be of great importance, depending on circumstances. Next, the Colonel pointed out how all the people of the world wished to maintain peace; and he was sure that the further development of the American nation would contribute to that end. He said, "I hope we may never be put into a position where our warships have to do their jobs. In 50 years or sooner, all these large naval forces may be a thing of the past." Colonel von Hecking-Colenbrander ended with words of praise for the American Navy.

Governor Hughes then asked Jonker Loudon, Ambassador from the Netherlands, to say a few words. The Governor introduced him with a short speech mentioning that Dutch ideas and ideals had left their imprint on life in America. Mr. Loudon responded by saying that now, more than any other time, he felt a sense of enjoyment standing on American soil. This was mainly because the Celebration came at a time when historical research had shown how the first Dutch colonists from old Holland had left their mark on the banks of the Hudson.

And although history does not support the view that the Dutch played a pivotal role in creating the American nation, Mr. Loudon argued that they did have a great influence on the country. "The acknowledgment of this influence makes every Dutchman feel good and their hearts fill with pride," Mr. Loudon said, "to see the orange, white, and blue flags throughout this magnificent city. It was under these colors that the first Dutch rebels under the command of William the Silent were able to free themselves from the Duke of Alva's Spanish tyranny. And next to this flag we see appropriately the red, white, and blue flag of the United States.

"These grand celebrations can only remind us of the struggles that our own small country went through 300 years ago to create a new freedom. In the United Netherlands a sense of freedom was created that spilled over into such areas as trade, science, and the arts. These principles of freedom were planted by the Dutch in virgin American soil. The English Separatists had found a refuge in Holland from the religious persecution to which they had been subjected in their own country; many of them departed for the New World, after either a long or short stay in Holland." Mr. Loudon also pointed to William Penn, whose mother was Dutch. He spoke of Henry Hudson and the first Dutch traders who settled on Manhattan and the famous Governors, doughty Wouter van Twiller, intolerant Willem Kieft, and the naughty Peter Stuyvesant. Mr. Loudon called it "a period in American history with many humorous inaccuracies, as depicted in the writings of Washington Irving and his Father Knickerbocker. You know," Mr. Loudon continued, "how during peacetime, our fierce colonial competitors took New Amsterdam by surprise. In the ensuing war, Dutch Admiral Evertsen was able to reconquer New Netherlands for a few years and how finally, with the treaty of Westminster, colonies were traded—with Surinam going to the Dutch and New Netherlands to the British."

Mr. Loudon followed with a description of Holland as being perfectly suited for the establishment of the international Court of Arbitration, and he finally expressed the wish "that the friendly relations between Holland and the United States would continue to improve and that the replica of the small but proud *Halve-Maen*, a gift from Holland to the American nation would, always remain the symbol of the ties between Holland and the United States."

Loud applause followed his words, which in a dignified manner closed this fifth day of the Hudson-Fulton Celebration in greater New York.

## EXTRACT FROM THE OFFICIAL NEW YORK STATE HISTORY (1910) OF THE HUDSON-FULTON CELEBRATION:

WEDNESDAY DAWNED CLEAR, and early in the morning a taciturn Wilbur Wright hastened to prepare his *Flyer* for the most dramatic demonstrations of powered flight to date. His contract with the Celebration Commission provided that some time between September 25 and October 9, to the extent of his ability and so far as weather and other conditions permitted, he would give New Yorkers a full demonstration of flight through the air. It would be a landmark in the history of worldwide aviation, the first public (non-military) exhibition of the *Flyer*, and everyone on the west side of Manhattan Island had a grandstand seat. The terms of Wright's agreement were sober and realistic. Wilbur was under no obligation to make any flight he deemed to be unreasonable or hazardous. He would be paid $15,000 for one or more flights exceeding either ten miles in distance or one hour in duration.

Wright arrived on Governor's Island, the staging place for all his activities, and those of Glenn Curtiss, shortly before 9:00 am. Even earlier that morning, Curtiss had made a flight of only 26 seconds duration, not witnessed by a single member of the Celebration's Aeronautics Committee. Wright's machine was pulled from its protective shed to the sand lot, placed on the launching monorail that swiveled due west into the wind and

**Plate 26: Glenn Curtiss at the controls of *June Bug*.**

over the harbor. The propeller was started. After listening to the rhythm of the engine for a moment with apparent satisfaction, Mr. Wright clambered into his historic machine. At 9:15 he gave the starting signal, leaving the ground rail in an easy glide. After two full circles over the airfield, he swung eastward over the Buttermilk Channel, following it to the northern end of Governor's Island. He turned westward and returned to his sandlot starting point, having completely encircled the island. He was in the air seven minutes and ten seconds and covered

**Plate 27: Wilbur Wright ready to fly for the Celebration.**

a distance of about two miles, his height varying from 40 to 100 feet. During the flight he was loudly saluted by the whistles of the tugs, steamboats, and factories from which he could be easily seen. An hour later he began a second flight, steering directly for the Statue of Liberty, accompanied by another din of steam whistles almost drowning out the sounds of countless cheering voices. Among the saluting vessels was the great ocean liner *Lusitania*,

just leaving New York Harbor for Liverpool.[2] Mr. Wright circled the Statue of
Liberty and returned to his Governor's Island airfield. At 5:00 pm he ascended
once more and remained aloft for 12 minutes. It was a remarkable occasion.

ON THE AFTERNOON of the same day, on a huge sloping rock face now contained within Fort Tryon Park, the American Scenic and Historic Preservation
Society unveiled a large bronze tablet donated by Cornelius Billings bearing this
inscription:

*ON THIS HILL STOOD*
*FORT TRYON*
*THE NORTHERN OUTWORK OF*
*FORT WASHINGTON*
*ITS GALLANT DEFENCE AGAINST*
*THE HESSIAN TROOPS*
*BY*
*THE MARYLAND AND VIRGINIA*
*REGIMENTS*
*16 NOVEMBER 1776*
*WAS SHARED BY*
*MARGARET CORBIN*
*THE FIRST AMERICAN WOMAN*
*TO TAKE A SOLDIERS PART*
*IN THE WAR FOR LIBERTY*

In that unfortunate battle, with the assistance of a turn-coat American soldier
named William Demont, the enemy captured over 2,500 Continental soldiers—
one-quarter of Washington's army.

GENERAL COMMEMORATIVE EXERCISES by universities, colleges, schools, museums and learned and patriotic societies were carried on throughout the entire
state. In New York City, under the auspices of the Board of Education, special
exercises were held in every elementary school. In the evening, illustrated lectures were given in 70 centers throughout the state. Aquatic sports, such as peaceful rowing races between the crews of foreign and American warships, and interstate contests between Naval Reserve crews were also held. Illustrated lectures
were presented in Tottenville, Stapleton, New Brighton, Fort Richmond, and
other Staten Island locations.

THE INCONSISTENCIES involved in refusing women a place at the Wednesday
evening banquet tables at the Waldorf Astoria, at an important international dinner saluting various concepts of political, religious, and economic emancipation,
appears to have exercised a sufficient number of guests, from both sides of the
Atlantic as to force the Commission to make formal defensive reply:
"Although the sentiment of the Commission were in favor of admitting ladies
to the table, the physical limitations of the banquet hall compelled the Committee
to restrict the ticket to gentlemen only.

So far as the boxes and the galleries permitted, however, the banquet was graced by the presence of the ladies."

Pshaw!

THE BALLROOM was dressed to produce the effect of a palace finished in delft-ware, with a large frieze representing a fleet of Viking ships also finished in delft blue and gold. At the north and south ends of the room, large paintings, each about 80 feet, long were placed. The one at the north end represented the Holland of Henry Hudson; the one at the south end represented the present-day New York Harbor, showing the Statue of Liberty, and the *Lusitania* coming up the bay, suggesting the voyages of Henry Hudson and the invention of Robert Fulton. Underneath these paintings, specially built out from the upper gallery, were models of the prows of the two ships. These were imbedded in masses of orange-colored chrysanthemums and asparagus vines. Moet & Chandon produced a special Hudson-Fulton cuvee of 1898 for the event.

# NOTES

[1]Despite almost a century of "suffragette agitation," the 19th Amendment to the U.S. Constitution was still a decade away.

[2]Less than six years later, the liner would be struck by a German torpedo and sent to the bottom of the Irish Sea, drowning 1,195 passengers.

# CHAPTER XV

## *NIEUWE ROTTERDAMSCHE COURANT*

New York, Thursday, September 30, 1909

Exclusive Dispatch

### THE HUDSON-FULTON CELEBRATION

ALL AMERICANS love parades, especially those of a military character. It was therefore no surprise that the small parade two days ago drew an estimated audience of one million people, while today's events were attended by close to two and a quarter million onlookers. Such a large and welcome attendance also created additional problems for the police.

Thanks to beautiful weather, today's events proved to be another great success. Almost 25,000 servicemen from both the Army and Navy paraded more than five miles from 110th Street, in the section called "Harlem," along the east side of Central Park and down Fifth Avenue to Washington Square. The parade, which started at 1:00 pm. this afternoon, finished around 5:30.

New York State's Governor Hughes was the guest of honor; President Taft could not be present due to an earlier commitment to the current World Exhibition on the Pacific Coast. As before, Governor Hughes was seated in the reviewing stand on Fifth Avenue and 41st Street in front of New York City's palatial new Public Library. The Governor was flanked on the left by Mayor George McClellan and on the right by Sir Edward Seymour, the British admiral. Seated around the Governor were Admiral Hans Ludwig von Koester, the commanding officer of the German squadron, the French commander Rear-Admiral Jean Paul Marie Le Pord, and other foreign military and civil dignitaries. The stands includ-

**Plate 28: Military Parade, West Point Cadets.**

ed Colonel van Hecking-Colenbrander of the *Utrecht* and one of the few surviving commanders of the American Civil War, 79-year-old General O. O. Howard,[1] a gentleman who had lost his right arm at the battle of Fair Oaks in Virginia in 1862.

The Governor's entire entourage stood as the U.S. veterans' contingent passed the reviewing stand. The first section of the parade was comprised of troops from the nations whose warships were participating in the festivities. At the front marched the U.S. sailors and marines, all greeted with cheers. They were followed by the Germans, striding before the Governor in their official parade step. Their impressive performance was greeted with applause. Then came the graceful French, looking quite different from the group that proceeded them. They, too, were greeted with cheers and applause, as were the military representatives of all the nations that followed.

Finally, after the Italians, Argentineans, and Mexicans had passed in review, the Dutch sailors and marines came in sight. Under the command of Lieutenant Verloop, they were impressive to watch, and as all the newspapers reported, they received great applause. Governor Hughes doffed his tall black hat many times as the soldiers passed the reviewing stand. They were followed by some thousand American sailors and marines, marching by in close ranks and warmly greeted with loud applause. Then came the well-received crews of all the participating warships, including six vessels of the U.S. Navy's special services unit, the equivalent of the Dutch Sea Militia.

Next in line were the cadets of the United States Military Academy at West Point, dressed in their traditional distinctive gray uniforms with white leather webbing across the chest, designed almost a century ago. These smartly-marching plebes were cheered by spectators all along the route. Around New York City, army cadets are very popular, but even more so are the naval cadets from their academy in Maryland. Following them came distinguished units from the cavalry, infantry, artillery, corps of engineers, signal corps, and so forth, all part of this country's national defense. Whereas in Holland one often looks skeptically at our militia army, here the National Guard is a source of great pride—maybe too much at times. There is a great interest over here for all things military.

The next part of the parade contained some interesting groups. The first were members of the Albany Burgess Corps, who had traveled down from the state capital. The second group was the Old Guard of the City of New York, which counts only notable New Yorkers among its members. They were dressed in two kinds of uniforms dating back a century or so; all wore tall bearskin hats. After them came the so-called Irish Volunteers, a type of militia to which only the sons of green Erin may belong. This section of the parade was followed by decorated war veterans. In addition to German, Polish, and other veterans, these ranks included members of the Grand Army of the Republic who fought in the 1861-65 American Civil War.

Making an interesting appearance in the parade was a billy goat led by sailors from the U.S.S. *Minnesota*. The animal is the mascot of its crew, or rather of the warship itself. Other nautical mascots included dogs, monkeys, cockatoos, raccoons, and so forth. It is interesting to see the competition between the crews of the decorated American warships. One of them boasts of its champion gunner, another of its top rower, still others of their champion boxer or soccer player.

---

### EXTRACT FROM THE OFFICIAL NEW YORK STATE HISTORY (1910) OF THE HUDSON-FULTON CELEBRATION:

THE MILITARY PARADE, participated in by the Federal troops of the Department of the East, the National Guard of the State of New York within New York City, the United States Marine Corps, the Naval Reserve, veterans organizations, and sailors from foreign warships followed the same route as that of the 28 September Historical Parade. It started at Central Park West and 110th Street, thence to 59th Street, to Fifth Avenue, and to Washington Square. Ambulance service and temporary hospitals were established along the route.

Unlike the previous Historical Parade, the procession started with military promptness at 1:00 pm. and reached the court of honor at 5th Avenue and 40th Street by 2:30 to pass in review for the Governor of New York and a distinguished company including United States and city officials. Never before had men under arms from so many nations set foot on New York soil. The British marines and sailors in straw hats and white leggings who led the first Division were given a magnificent reception, the spectators rising en masse and cheering wildly. Nothing could have more strikingly demonstrated the ameliorating influences of time than this demonstration. (By coincidence, it took place where, 133 years before, American and British troops were engaged in hostile combat.)

There were no serious accidents or parade interruptions except for the necessary movement on certain crosstown trolley lines. The police controlled the crowds skillfully, patiently, and effectively.

ONGOING FESTIVITIES included: Aquatic sports and motorboat races in five classes; a banquet at the huge Ferry Terminal Building at St. George, Staten Island; a reception at the Brooklyn Academy of Music; arrival of *Half-Moon* and *Clermont* and their escorts at Ossining, and their departure for Peekskill by way of Haverstraw Bay and the west bank of the Hudson. At Cornwall, commemorative exercises took place at the public schools.

# NOTES

[1]Brigadier General Oliver Otis Howard was the prominent Maine abolitionist who later gave his name to Howard University. A West Point graduate, he performed Civil War service from First Manassas to Sherman's March through Georgia. At the end of the war he was placed in charge of the government's Freedmen's Bureau, encouraging and assisting tens of thousands of former slaves to make new lives for themselves in the United States. Howard later led the U.S. Army in its war with the western Native Americans. He died a few weeks after the end of the Hudson-Fulton Celebration.

# C H A P T E R   XVI

## *NIEUWE ROTTERDAMSCHE COURANT*

New York, Friday, October 1, 1909

Exclusive Dispatch

### THE HUDSON-FULTON CELEBRATION

IT FEELS LIKE THE FESTIVITIES are all happening at the same time as opposed to following one another. There are numerous invitations to events, dinners and balls, and so forth. Last night a Hudson-Fulton dinner was held on Staten Island, with another at the same time at the Plaza Hotel, both hosted by the Dutch guests. We were also all invited for an evening of dancing and music in Brooklyn. It did not come as a surprise therefore, that during the afternoon in Newburgh, there were apologizes for the absence of the Dutch guests. Said Mr. F. C. Stoop, a member of the Netherlands delegation, provoking thunderous laughter, the number of invitations has almost killed our Dutch guests—not quite, but close.

This morning at 6 am, we left our lodgings and proceeded by subway to Riverside Park on the Hudson. We boarded the steam launch which ferried us out to H.M.S. *Utrecht*. It was a beautiful morning, with the sun awakening the river from its dreams; a golden mist that covered the water slowly evaporated. While all the other warships remained downriver, the *Utrecht* had the honor of sailing upriver to Newburgh. According to Mr. David Roche, the ship's American river pilot, it was the first time that a foreign armored ship had sailed that far up the Hudson.[1]

People on board the ship were very enthusiastic about our trip, which en

**Plate 29: Naval Parade at Newburgh, October 1, 1909.**

route passed the British warships, *Portsmouth, Inflexible, Drake, Argyle,* and *Duke of Edinburgh,* followed by a long line of American warships that eventually anchored in the middle of the river. Every time the *Utrecht* passed another war vessel, a maritime salute was sounded and its honor guard presented arms. This was answered with counter salutes, and the *Utrecht*'s crew singing the "Wilhelmus van Nassauen." One cannot easily forget the sound of this familiar music floating across the water on this beautiful morning in such a faraway country. We had hardly overcome this emotion when we became aware of more beauty all around us. Sailing up the Hudson, we first passed the steeply rising Palisades, then the wooded mountainous terrain with its fall foliage, presenting an unforgettable picture under the clear October sky. We know that many letters will soon find their way home, telling of our wonderful trip along this American Rhine, mentioned by so many poets and to our great pride, carrying Hudson's name. The Dutch were as friendly on land as they were on the water. There was no end to the cheering and the waving of flags coming from ships and boats, loaded with spectators, as they were passed by the *Utrecht* as it sped along at 14 knots. From every commercial craft, passenger boat, and even the smallest motorboat flew the *oranje, blanje, bleu.*

At West Point, where the landscape becomes wilder and more spectacular, old and young had come together on the banks of the river to view the spectacle. Loud cheers went up as the *Utrecht* passed. As we arrived at the military academy, a 21-gun salute sounded, followed by the hoisting of the Dutch and American flags. But where were all the young cadets who only yesterday had paraded so

**Plate 30: *Half-Moon* and *Clermont* in Newburgh Bay.**

impressively in their snow white pants, dressy gray jackets and shakos? Still asleep? We don't know. What we do know is that none of them showed up.

Though some enthusiasm was missing at West Point, it was doubly available in all the other places that our warship passed on its stately route up the majestic river. Around 12 o'clock we arrived in Newburgh in time for lunch. The *Halve-Maen*, which had sailed upriver yesterday, was already tied up at one of the docks. The little ship looked so tiny next to the solemn gray American warships. But its Dutch tricolor fluttered briskly in the breeze, coloring the water's surface.

After lunch, we journalists had little opportunity for reflection on American style; a 21-gun salute interrupted our musings, reminding us that the Hudson-Fulton festivities were continuing outside the *Utrecht*'s wardroom. The *Halve-Maen* paused by the Newburgh reviewing stand to allow Hudson and his mate Juet to disembark. Meanwhile the *Clermont*, with Robert Fulton, made a similar transfer.

We arrived just in time to see General Woodford officially introduce both ships to the Upper-Hudson celebration Committee. A short time later we were transported by motorcar to the Newburgh City Club, where we were all officially greeted. Instead of shaking the Admiral's hand in a formal reception line, I interviewed Mr. Benthem, a member of the committee, asking him about the final destination—or disposition—of the *Halve-Maen* after the Celebration. He gave me no specific answer, but it was clear that the oft proposed anchorage in Brooklyn's Prospect Park lake was not in the cards. He said that this Dutch present to the people of New York would either take its place on the lake in Central Park or, as we had been told earlier, in a still to be built special Half Moon Park somewhere up the Hudson, even perhaps above Albany. Mr. Benthem did not think that transportation to Central Park would be feasible, because the ship could not squeeze under the city's "El" tracks. But if New Yorkers really wanted the ship in Central Park, they would have to find a way to get it there, even digging out the streets to make it fit.

We really saw very little of the actual festivities in Newburgh, only lots of people, dusty roads, and steep cobblestone streets leading down to the waterfront, on which you could easily break your neck.

MUCH LATER, softly rocking in the West Shore Railroad parlor car that carried us back to New York City, we reminisced about our beautiful trip this morning. And with this I must say good-bye to the upriver Hudson-Fulton festivities. Even though the program is not finished, what is left is of less interest and importance, and I would run the risk of repeating myself. In addition, I more or less reached the goal I had set.

What I had in mind with these reports was to give readers an objective picture of the facts surrounding the Hudson-Fulton festivities. And insofar as the Henry Hudson part was concerned, to show that it was a special tribute, not to the British or Germans, but to that famous navigator and all the sturdy Dutchmen who were our bold, undaunted forefathers.

---

EXTRACT FROM THE OFFICIAL NEW YORK STATE HISTORY (1910)
OF THE HUDSON-FULTON CELEBRATION:

EVENTS: Naval Parade from New York City to Newburgh. Brooklyn Historical Pageant, 54 floats proceeding from the Memorial Arch at the entrance to Prospect Park at Eastern Parkway. A civic and historical parade at Cornwall with floats representing progress in the Hudson Valley. Fireworks accompanied the arrival of the fleet at Newburgh Bay. Landing of sailors and marines and parade to reviewing stand at the Newburgh Courthouse. Complimentary shore dinner for 5,000 paraders. Evening illumination of city and vessels in the bay. Additional fireworks.

# NOTES

[1]For a week in October, 1777, during the American Revolution, a small British naval squadron carrying soldiers actually penetrated as far north as Kingston, then the capital of New York State, and burned it to the ground. In 1778, a massive iron chain strung across the river at West Point successfully blocked the Hudson to any further British naval incursions.

# CHAPTER XVII

## *NIEUWE ROTTERDAMSCHE COURANT*

New York, Saturday, October 2, 1909

Exclusive Dispatch

### THE HUDSON-FULTON CELEBRATION

THE FESTIVITIES have ended with a nighttime Carnival Parade. It was the greatest show of all. After so many days of ceremonial celebration, there was a general public expression of joy and ultimate cheerfulness, following which New York will revert to its normal bustling character. Again the weather cooperated to the fullest. The scheduling allowed many who had not been able to attend the celebrations during the day because of work an opportunity to enjoy themselves at night. People were generally disappointed that New York State's Governor Hughes never made good on his promise to declare the three most important days legal holidays, even though the organizing committee had more than once made reference to the promise. His apology still has not been issued.

The parade gave the impression of a glittering, rippling stream of variegated lights flowing over dark pavements covered with people who continued to cheer. It was a lot shorter than the Military Parade on 30 September, but it still took until midnight before it was all over, even though it had started at eight o'clock that evening. It was a more impressive parade and seemed better organized than the Historical Parade of 25 September.

The procession left exactly on time, again from 110th Street and Central Park West in Harlem. The 50 floats, manned by more than 14,000 members of an assortment of German, Swiss, and Austrian fraternal organizations, traveled without any significant delay along the western and southern side of this beautiful park, crossing Park Plaza at 59th Street and turning south on Fifth Avenue. That avenue all the way to Washington Square has always been known as the area "where the rich live." A slow transformation, however, is taking place near 50th Street, which is becoming commercial. During the last few months, buildings formerly occupied by wealthy families have been replaced by first-class shops and massive office buildings, whose construction scaffolds provided an opportunity for many onlookers to watch the parade from on high.

It certainly was a day of celebration by the people and for the people, in the greatest sense of Lincoln's words. During the day, thousands of costumed schoolchildren paraded with their flags, while nighttime provided adults with their opportunity to celebrate, irrespective of age or social class. The happy and festive mood along Fifth Avenue lasted past midnight without any rough behavior.

Every building along the parade route was lit up, and the garlands of electrical bulbs turned night into day. An estimated 1.5 to 3 million people attended. About twice as many people were present today as there were for all the previous parades. Everywhere along the route Bengal lights[1] as well as the light of multicolored torches carried by the marchers illuminated a million cheering faces.

Art, history, folklore, and legends were the sources for the parade's tastefully designed floats, which drew cheers as they passed by. But the greatest effect was achieved by those participants who were not in uniform but who were all dressed in either white or red dominoes.[2] The procession came to its full glory in front of the honorary reviewing stand erected in front of the Public Library at 41st Street.

Mayor McClellan, together with Herman Ridder, of the New York *Staats-Zeitung* and guiding light for the organizing committee, were at the head of the procession. Mr. Ridder must have felt the greatest satisfaction with the outcome of all his plans for the Celebration.

The Hudson-Fulton festivities were certainly a great success in virtually all respects. Holland can look back with pride and gratitude to the many gestures of goodwill made by the Americans toward the Dutch. But in addition to the gratitude that we feel toward today's New Yorkers, there is a different feeling of respectful admiration for the generations of seafarers and merchants who in the first half of the 17th century created an offshoot of the Republic of the United Netherlands on this side of the ocean.

---

EXTRACT FROM THE OFFICIAL NEW YORK STATE HISTORY (1910)
OF THE HUDSON-FULTON CELEBRATION:

IN THE AFTERNOON a fete was held on the grounds of Columbia University. It brought together most of the officers of the foreign and American warships, with their interpreters, offering them an opportunity to meet representative men and women of New York in a freer social atmosphere.

Plate 31: Sketches for Carnival Parade floats.

ON THE TRAIN ride back to New York City from the outdoor celebratory lunch-eon at Newburgh, the newspapermen in the press car passed by the Stony Point station of the New York Ontario & Western Railroad. Earlier in the day, Stony Point enjoyed its own celebration. At noon, the commission opened memorial fes-tivities at the shoreline battlefield opposite Verplank, which is on the east bank of the Hudson River and at the southern gateway to the Highlands.

The center of interest was the dedication of a large arch of native rock, erected by the Daughters of the American Revolution and the American Scenic and Historic Preservation Society to commemorate the total American victory at this spot, 16 July 1779, when Stony Point was redeemed from British occupation, albeit tem-porarily.[3]

CHILDREN'S FESTIVALS were held this day in public parks throughout New York City. They consisted of historical plays and folk dances in costume, with appro-priate music.

THE FOLLOWING EVENTS took place in the different boroughs:
Bronx Borough: athletic meet at Crotona Park Playing Field.
Manhattan: evening Carnival Parade, following the same route as the September 28th Historical Parade. It represented, on moving vehicles, allegorical, mytholog-ical, and historical scenes. The great Historical Parade and most of the other fea-tures of the Celebration dealt mainly with facts of history and of material and social progress. The Carnival pageant, however, dealt with different aspects of culture, the beautiful imagery of the poetry, song and drama of all civilized nations.
Richmond Borough: a pageant including 25 floats from the Manhattan  28 Sep-tember Historical Parade, with about 5,000 paraders.
Yonkers: amateur rowing and canoe races.
Newburgh: farewell to the fleet, a portion returning to New York, with shallower draft vessels accompanying the *Half-Moon* and *Clermont* farther upriver to Poughkeepsie. Motorboat races in four classes.

LATER, addressing a crowd of celebrants at Kingston, Governor Charles Evans Hughes, casting an oracular eye on his political career (in the presidential election of 1916, he lost to Woodrow Wilson by 600,000 votes), said: "The best exhibit in this whole Celebration is the people of the State of New York. In the metropolis, where are represented all nations and where are gathered together scions of all the races in a cosmopolitan community the like of which has never been seen upon this earth, there were, during the preceding week, the largest crowds in the history of the city, and at the same time, good order, good humor, happiness, con-tentment and almost an entire absence of anything to give offense or to bring a stain upon the fair fame of our great City of New York."

ON THE FOLLOWING DAY, Sunday, October 3, religious services were held throughout the Hudson Valley. There was a sacred concert at Carnegie Hall by the People's Choral Union and instrumentalists from Walter Damrosch's New York Symphony Society under the leadership of Frank Damrosch.

# NOTES

[1] A flare emitting a steady blue light, usually used for signaling.

[2] Loose cloaks or robes with wide sleeves and a hood.

[3] The attack, past midnight, was brilliantly executed by General "Mad Anthony" Wayne, crying "The Fort's our own!" A barge laden with captured British muskets and rifles, plus some heavy artillery that Washington ordered immediately shipped to West Point, unfortunately capsized in midstream.

# CHAPTER XVIII

## *NIEUWE ROTTERDAMSCHE COURANT*

New York, Monday, October 4, 1909

Exclusive Dispatch

### THE HUDSON-FULTON CELEBRATION

THE PARTY OVER, New York City is having trouble getting back to the daily grind. There are still a number of dinners and parties to come, which we shall not report on. Of special interest was Saturday's big party for New York's schoolchildren, which signaled the official closing of the Hudson-Fulton festivities. About half a million children, in over 50 different local parks up and down the river, took part in a variety of activities, many of which were presented in costume. It was also the last night that both the warships and pleasure craft were illuminated.

A likely result of the celebration in New York will be that Riverside Drive, the boulevard along the Hudson River opposite the Palisades, will receive a monument in memory of Fulton. The proposed monument, a marble tomb containing Fulton's remains, will be carved into the rocks on the edge of the river. It will be in the company of such great New York structures as Grant's Tomb, the Library of Columbia University, Barnard College, the Cathedral of St. John the Divine, and so forth. A magnificent arch will give entry to the monument. Funds are now being raised for its construction.[1]

AS MENTIONED EARLIER, the Dutch Chamber of Commerce, in connection with the Hudson-Fulton festivities, has published a booklet about the Dutch in New

Netherland and the United States. Both spine and title page show a handsome vignette of the *Halve-Maen*. Around it are the words "The Netherland Chamber of Commerce in America." The text was composed and translated into English by our Secretary of Commerce, Mr. T. Greidanus. The motto is borrowed from a well-known work of Adriaen van der Donck, who wrote in 1656: "New Netherland is a beautiful place where it seems easier for people to make a living than anywhere in the world." Unfortunately, in his text the too brief mention of King William I is historically unfair; he was one of the principal founders of Dutch independence. Of interest, though, is Mr. Greidanus's mention of Dutch settlements in Iowa, Michigan, and Illinois (Chicago and surrounding towns), as well as California, Philadelphia, Patterson, New Jersey, and even Sayville, Long Island.

The importance of the Dutch in the United States becomes clear when one learns that there are 16 Dutch newspapers currently printed here—although, surprisingly, none of them in New York. In closing, Mr. Greidanus provided some important warnings and advice to those who would like to emigrate to the United States. The essence of these is: If you don't like things American, you may be certain that America will not change because you do not approve. On the contrary, he said, America is likely to change you. Grumbling and dissatisfaction with things as they are will only make you unhappy and unfit, but the world will go on just the same. Once you come to America, be an American.

*****************************

THUS ENDS the formal file of Rudolph's dispatches to the readers of the *Nieuwe Rotterdamsche Courant*. The Celebration, however, continued for another five days with festivities up and down the river, from New York City to the head of navigation, near Cohoes.

UNDOUBTEDLY, THE MOST important event of the day was Wilbur Wright's fourth and most spectacular flight from Governors Island to a point about 1,000 feet north of Grant's Tomb, and return. The previous day, Glenn Curtiss had made an unofficial flight of 45 seconds. Heading for the Statue of Liberty, Curtiss momentarily lost control of his aeroplane and immediately returned to the ground, and today began packing up his flying machine for shipment to his next demonstration, in St. Louis. For Wilbur Wright weather conditions were again almost ideal. Two American flags were affixed to the front rudder of the *Flyer*, and a life preserver was placed near his feet. The aeronaut left the ground at 9:33 am, and headed directly up the Hudson River. Conflicting air currents caused the aeroplane to waver a little in its course, but all was well. Hearing the factory and ship's whistles, crowds of people rushed to roofs and other points of vantage to salute the "man-bird" on his historic flight. He reached the southern end of the line of the great international war fleet that stretched ten miles north from 42nd Street. From

**Plate 32: Wilbur Wright in flight over Upper Bay.**

these death-dealing warships, any of which Wright could have destroyed with a single bomb, cheering sailors gazed in wonder and admiration at the daring aviator. Passing beyond Grant's Tomb, Wright made a semicircular turn towards the New Jersey shore. The maneuver, which occupied about three-quarters of a minute, was executed at a height of from 100 to 150 feet. On the return trip, with the wind at his back, Wright reached the Governor's Island airfield at 10:26 am. He had been in the air 33 minutes and 33 seconds. The total distance covered by Wilbur Wright in his half-ton *Flyer* was reckoned to be about 20 miles. It was one of the most perilous air flights made up to that time. Wright said that air currents diverted by Manhattan's skyscrapers were bothersome, and particularly a puff which he experienced at 23rd Street, where he was flying lower than the height of the new Metropolitan Insurance tower. In the afternoon an unfortunate accident to the *Flyer* precluded further air voyages. At 3:30 pm, the aeroplane was brought out to the launching rail. After nine unsuccessful attempts to start the propeller, a sudden explosion blew off a cylinder head. Mr. Wright spread out his hands and said simply, "No more flights in New York." He had vindicated the confidence placed in him by the Commission's Aeronautics Committee.

Within a month, the Wrights established their first flying school at College Park, Maryland.

AT YONKERS there was a parade of historical floats and military and civic organizations, reviewed by Governor Hughes. At Poughkeepsie, a military, civic, industrial, and historical parade including 20 floats was followed by a banquet and reception again honoring Governor Hughes, who said: "The money that has been spent on this celebration has not been wasted. We have too few opportunities in this country to come together when there are no partisan issues to be discussed, or individual prejudices to be incurred, or candidacies to be fostered—but we are all united, emphasizing our unity and sinking our differences, in order that America may be great because its people are inspired to justice and appreciation of the ideals of the Republic.

"I say to you, my friends, it has been worthwhile, and we are all together in this great State of New York, knowing more of our glorious past, more confident of the future, than we would have been if we had not worked so hard to give an adequate representation of our joy in our progress."

EDWARD HAGAMAN HALL, secretary and chief publicist for the American Committee, closed the book on the Celebration by remarking, "The Hudson-Fulton Celebration was a jubilee of happiness. The nation was at peace with the world, civil concord blessed our people at home, material prosperity abounded. Even man's evil propensity seemed to be suspended, and the best qualities of human nature had come to the surface. For it is a literal fact that during the two weeks of the Celebration in New York City, there were fewer homicides, fewer suicides, and less crime generally than in any other equal period of the year. There were also fewer accidents and a lower general death rate than usual. There was seemingly nothing to mar the happiness of the occasion, and the people practically abandoned themselves for a fortnight to a rational festival of patriotic sentiment."

An important result of the Hudson-Fulton Celebration was the manner in which it swelled local pride in the valley's history. It was the precursor of the civic and conservationist efforts that followed. The latest, the Hudson Valley Greenway, reflects the ideas and actions of a group of dedicated men and women whose thinking was inspired by the great 1909 Hudson-Fulton Celebration.

# NOTES

[1]The Fulton Memorial was never built.

# CHAPTER IX

# POSTSCRIPTS

*Each age is a dream that is dying,*
*Or one that is coming to birth.*
　　　　　　　　—Ode by A.W. E. O'SHAUGHNESSY

WHAT FICKLE FATE eventually befell the 1909 facsimiles of the *Half-Moon* and *Clermont*? That is the question most often asked by New Yorkers when, for the first time, they learn the story of their city's great Hudson-Fulton Celebration. In the run-up to the event, it was generally assumed (but not decided) that the replicated ships would claim a permanent if anachronistic home in the middle of the Central Park Lake. This charmingly bucolic disposition was dropped when it was noted that the *Half-Moon's* extensive rigging (unlike Cleopatra's Needle) could not easily fit under Manhattan's "El" tracks. Oh, what an opportunity was missed!

An alternate decision was made to place the *Half-Moon* in the custody of the newly formed Palisades Interstate Park Commission, to be permanently anchored in scenic Popolopen Creek, just above Bear Mountain on the Hudson River, where it could capture the imagination of thousands of picnicking New Yorkers. On Friday, July 15, 1910, the transfer was accomplished with an admonition that this unusual Dutch present to the citizens of New York be given decent care. The Hudson-Fulton Commission was quite specific regarding the obligations of the ship's new stewards. By unanimous vote, they required:

> First: That the *Half-Moon* shall ordinarily be kept floating upon the Hudson River in the State of New York.
> Second: that the Commissioners of the Palisades Interstate Park, New York Commission, shall keep in repair, protect and preserve the vessel with the utmost possible care.
> Third: that the public shall be permitted to visit and inspect the vessel under suitable regulations; and

Fourth: That with the approval of the Governor of the State of New York, the vessel be permitted to take part in public ceremonies relating to science and navigation or to the Hudson River.

Thereafter, a view of the *Half-Moon* in Popolopen Creek became a high spot for visitors to Bear Mountain from all over the world.

**Plate 33: *Half-Moon* in Popolopen Creek, 1924.**
**Bear Mountain Bridge under construction in background.**

But only six years later, it had become clear that the Palisades Interstate Park Commission was not fulfilling its obligations. In a letter from James Sullivan, Director of Archives and History at the New York State Education Department, to George W. Perkins, President of the Palisades Interstate Park Commission, Mr. Sullivan complained that the present appearance and condition of the *Half-Moon* was a disgrace, virtually abandoned and prey to the weather and ice in the Hudson River. Mr. Perkins referred the matter to the park's General Manager, Major W. A. Welch, who investigated and replied in an internal memo: "At the moment, the *Half-Moon* is lying on the mud with her bow about two feet below her proper water line because the ice, which two weeks ago froze very heavily around her bow, pulled the corking [caulk] out of the planking and we cannot get at her to re-cork these joints as long as the ice remains in the river. We have pumped her out and floated her a half dozen times in the last ten days but she fills up and settles each night and since she is in a better and safer condition as she now lies, we have determined to do nothing with her until the ice is out of the river when we can again pump her out and recork the seams. She has not been injured in any way. All of the things of value which were in the ship were taken and stored sometime ago."

To rebut Sullivan's charges, Perkins immediately wrote to William A. Orr, Secretary to the Governor: "I do not think I will answer this [Sullivan's] letter, as it is so insulting and needlessly offensive. The facts are that the *Half-Moon* has been anchored at Bear Mountain for two or three years. The State of New York has refused to allow us any money with which to maintain her, although we have requested it. It has been cut out of our appropriations, so that we have had to maintain her out of other funds. Nevertheless, we have kept a man on her both winter and summer, at a cost of $720 per year and we have made repairs without any allowance from the state." Perkins then went on to explain the actual location and current condition of the replica.

By 1920, the Holland Society of New York City was sufficiently exercised over the decayed condition of the symbolic vessel to question New York's apparently failing stewardship. The society Secretary had sent the Palisades Park management a resolution by his group reminding everyone of past promises unfulfilled. The Palisades Park Commission secretary, J. DuPratt White, responded:

> The vessel has been for some years moored in the mouth of Popolopen Creek. The railroad drawbridge crossing the entrance from the river into that Creek has now been permanently closed and the vessel, therefore, is shut off from the river. The Commission regards this as fortunate, however, rather than unfortunate. She lies in quiet water and is safe.
>
> "The Commission has no funds available for her upkeep and repairs, but it does maintain a watchman of late, who is supposed to and, as far as the Commission is able to ascertain, has protected the vessel from vandals.
>
> "The Park Commissioners feel that the best permanent disposition of this craft would be to raise her on a concrete base above the waters of Popolopen Creek and have her there permanently set at such a height above the tidal water that she would not readily be accessible to vandals who might reach her in small boats, and yet would be within view of the public, and the Commissioners have instructed their Engineer to prepare an estimate of what such disposition would cost, including also the scraping and painting of the vessel. I have not yet received that estimate, but as soon as I do, I will take pleasure in transmitting it to you with the thought and hope, which the Commission entertains, that your Society may be able, provided the amount is reasonable, to suggest some method by which it can be financed.

General Manager Welch's estimate of the funds required to put the *Half-Moon* in proper shape was $2,300. But even that figure proved too high for the Holland Society to underwrite.

In 1924 the Hudson River Day Line was approached by the Parks Commission to take over all maintenance and financial responsibility for the *Half-Moon*. The Day Line demurred. Last resort was the New York State Legislature. But they and Governor Al Smith showed little interest, even in the boom times of the 20s, whereupon the Parks Commission looked favorably at an application from Mayor Daniel J. Cosgro of Cohoes, New York[1] that the *Half-Moon* be removed to that Hudson River city as a permanent memorial. The State Legislature passed an enabling act "releasing to the city of Cohoes all the right, title and interest in and to the vessel *Half-Moon*. The People of the State of New York, represented in Senate and Assembly, do enact as follows:

"The State hereby grants, transfers and releases to the city of Cohoes all its right, title and interest in and to the vessel Half-Moon, now at the mouth of Popolopen Creek near Bear Mountain, in consideration and on condition that the city of Cohoes shall remove the same to such city. This act shall take effect immediately."

In Cohoes' East Side Park, the "drydocked" ship remained for almost a decade, rotting away until 9 September 1933, when it was set afire in a final act of vandalism. Thus perished the gift of the people of the Netherlands to the people of New York.

WHAT HAPPENED to the *Clermont* (nee `North River Steamboat')?

In a letter dated March 20, 1936, addressed to Mr. J. DuPratt White, President, Palisades Interstate Park Commission, Oscar K. Goll, Managing Editor, WPA Federal Writers' Projects, asks: "In the course of gathering material for the *New York Guide Book*, we would like to know if you have any information concerning the replica of the first river steamboat *Clermont*, which was used during the Hudson-Fulton Celebration here in 1909." Four days later, Mr. Gol had his answer from Major Welch: "I haven't the slightest idea as to what became of the replica."

RUDOLPH DIAMANT loved and cherished his acquired United States citizenship, his wife, the family they were raising, and the increasing complexity and responsibility of his work. They moved to an apartment on West 76th street, around the corner from the American Museum of Natural History and the New-York Historical Society—two learning facilities that would be hard to beat in any culture, and in which I spent many happy days. Only a single avenue lay between our home and Central Park, a triple scoop for growing up. But sadness lay ahead. In the early 1920s, while vacationing with his family along the Jersey shore, Rudolph contracted viral encephalitis, an inflammation of the brain. Symptoms included "partial paralysis, headaches and seizures, progressive impairment or loss of intellectual ability and speech." Many sufferers developed what came to be known as post-encephalitic parkinsonism. My father was among them.

After a long and wasting illness, Rudolph chose suicide by leaping from a high apartment house window in upper Manhattan.

It was Seder night, 1927. I was four years old.

It was only 18 years after all the hoopla on the Hudson had passed into history.

---

The New York Times
Sunday, April 17, 1927

---

### LEAPS EIGHT STORIES TO DEATH

Insurance Man Went to Mother-in-law's Home for Passover Service

Rudolph Diamant, a 42-year-old insurance adjuster living at 59 West 76th Street, went with his wife last night to the home of his mother-in-law, Mrs. Dora Bloom, on the eighth floor of the apartment house at 174 Lenox Avenue, to take part in the Jewish Passover services.

A few minutes after his arrival, Diamant walked into the front room, and according to police, jumped from a balcony into the street. His body narrowly missed several passersby as it hit the sidewalk.

Patrolman Harry Highstrant, of the West 123rd Street Station, notified Harlem Hospital, and Dr. I. Cohen pronounced Diamant dead. The police were told that Diamant recently had a nervous breakdown.

# NOTES

[1]A small industrial town northeast of Albany, about halfway up the Hudson watershed.

**Plate 34: Rudolph and Lincoln Diamant,
Avon-by-the-Sea, New Jersey, 1926.**

# ABOUT THE AUTHOR

LINCOLN DIAMANT is a Hudson Valley historian and author. Graduating from Columbia in 1943, he spent much of his professional life in broadcast communications. He has written several books on the American Revolution including *Chaining the Hudson* which tells the strategic role of our great river during the War of Independence. The book won the annual Westchester Library Association Award. Mr. Diamant is an honorary board member of the Fort Montgomery Battle Site Association, and an authority on the transfer of royalist land titles by the New York State Commissioners of Forfeiture. He has also written a biography of Bernard Romans, the Continental Army captain who undertook the first fortification of West Point—called by both sides the "Key of America." Other books include *Stamping Our History, The Story of the United States Portrayed on its Postage Stamps, Yankee Doodle Days*—a collection of essays on the war—and *Revolutionary Women*—82 short biographies of mainly unknown females who played a part in the conflict. He recently finished editing an illustrated history of Westchester's Teatown Lake Reservation, of which he was the first president. He is presently at work on *DIVE! The Story of David Bushnell and His Remarkable 1776 Submarine (and Torpedo)*. It tells how a secretive Yankee genius, David Bushnell, set his sights on the Royal Navy and built the world's first submarine to carry the world's first torpedo. For New York State, he created the traveling historical exhibit, *"Defending the Hudson, 1775-1783,"* currently on display at the Visitor's Center at West Point, helping celebrate the Military Academy's 200th anniversary.

# ABOUT THE PUBLISHER

PURPLE MOUNTAIN PRESS is a publishing company committed to producing the best original books of regional interest as well as bringing back into print significant older works. It also publishes and imports maritime books under its Harbor Hill imprint. For a free catalog, write Purple Mountain Press, Ltd., P.O. Box 309, Fleischmanns, NY 12430-0309, or call 845-254-4062, or fax 845-254-4476, or email purple@catskill.net.
http://www.catskill.net/purple